The Bush Theatre
presents the world premiere of

C000050621

I Like Mine With A Kiss

by Georgia Fitch

14 February – 17 March 2007

Cast

(in alphabetical order)

Jean **Linda Broughton**
Louise **Michelle Butterly**
Jim **Ruairi Conaghan**
Annie **Heather Craney**
Mathieu **Andrew French**
Freya **Jade Williams**

Director **Mike Bradwell**
Designer **Libby Watson**
Lighting Designer **James Farncombe**
Sound Designer **David Benke**
Assistant Director **Nadia Latif**
Production Manager **Spencer New**
Deputy Stage Manager **Emily Peake**

I Like Mine With A Kiss received its world premiere performance at The Bush Theatre on 14 February 2007.

Linda Broughton *Jean*

Linda's theatre credits include Esther in *The Safari Party* (New Vic Theatre, Stoke), Mrs Sarti in *The Life of Galileo*, Ann Putnam and Sarah Good in *The Crucible*, Heather in *Racing Demon*, Gwenda in *Absence of War* and *Murmuring Judges* (Birmingham Repertory Theatre), Sylvia in *Ballroom* for De Le Warr Pavillion (Tour), Pam in *Hoxton Story* (The Red Room), Miss Prism in *The Importance of Being Earnest*, *My Mother Said I Never Should* (Royal Theatre, Northampton), *When The Wind Blows* (Southwark Playhouse), *Northanger Abbey* and *Forty Years On* (Northcott Theatre, Exeter), *Sugar Dollies* (Gate Theatre), *Rookery Nook* (Greenwich Theatre), *Small Poppies* (Young Vic), *Macbeth* (Crucible Theatre, Sheffield), *Caucasian Chalk Circle* (Birmingham Repertory Theatre). Linda has also appeared in repertory seasons at The Octagon Theatre, Bolton, Citizens' Theatre, Glasgow, Birmingham Repertory Theatre and The Crucible Theatre, Sheffield.

On television Linda's credits include *Doctors, Waking The Dead, Casualty, Paul Merton: Does China Exist?, Hetty Wainthropp Investigates, Fist of Fun, Chandler and Co, Roughnecks, Knowing Me Knowing You, A Dark Adapted Eye, Carrie and Barry, Men Behaving Badly, Wycliffe, Expert Witness, The Bill, Firm Friends* and *How We Used to Live*.

Linda's film credits include *Bridget Jones's Diary, Sliding Doors* and *Watch That Man*.

Michelle Butterly *Louise*

Michelle trained at Central School Of Speech And Drama.

Theatre includes *Speaking Like Magpies, A New Way to Please You, Believe What You Will* and *Thomas More* (RSC / Stratford and Trafalgar Studios), *Gone to Earth* (Shared Experience / Tour), *The People are Friendly* (Royal Court), *The Servant to Two Masters* (RSC and West End), *Safe* (Carob Theatre / Tie Tour), *Road, Shakers* (Wolsey Theatre, Ipswich), *Peggy Buck* (Belgrade Theatre, Coventry), *End of the Food Chain* (Stephen Joseph Theatre), *Laundry Room at the Hotel Madrid* (Gate Theatre), *Lent* (Belgrade Studio, Coventry) and *Gaslight* (Theatr Clwyd).

Television includes *No Angels II, Eyes Down, Dangerfield, Pie in the Sky, Hetty Wainthrop Investigates, Soldier Soldier, St Clare, The Echo, Heartbeat* and *Casualty*.

Film includes *Chromophobia*.

Ruairi Conaghan *Jim*

Theatre includes *The Factory Girls* (Arcola Theatre), *A Thousand Yards* (Southwark Playhouse), *Port Authority* (Liverpool Everyman), *Someone To Watch Over Me* (Northampton Theatre), *Scenes From The Big Picture, Peer Gynt* (National Theatre), *Trust* (National Theatre / Royal Court), *Philadelphia Here I Come*

(TMA nomination for Best Supporting Actor; Belfast and USA tour/Wyndhams Theatre), *Tearing The Loom, A Midsummer Night's Dream, Put Out That Light* (Lyric, Belfast), *Green, Orange And Pink, Drill Hall Elegies* (Kings Head Theatre), *Othello, School For Scandal, The White Devil* (Everyman Theatre), *Fall From Grace* (Liverpool Playhouse), *Ruffian On The Stair, Rough Justice, Box* (Northcott, Exeter), *Sinking, That Driving Ambition* (Replay Northern Irish tour) and *Blood, Sweat And Tears* (Big Telly Northern Irish tour).

Television includes *The Catherine Tate Show, Waking The Dead, Silent Witness, The Bill, Frances Tuesday, Murphy's Law, Do The Right Thing, All Things Bright And Beautiful, Made In Heaven* and *Cuchullain*.

Film includes *It's A Goat's Life, An Officer From France* and *Walk With Me*.

Radio includes *The Man From God Knows Where* and *The Lonely Passion Of Judith Hearne* (BBC Radio 4).

Heather Craney *Annie*

Theatre includes *Sugar Mummies, Stoning Mary* (Royal Court), *Still Life / Astonished Heart* (Liverpool Playhouse), *Blue Remembered Hills* (National Theatre Studio), *Romeo and Juliet, All That Trouble We Had* (New Vic, Stoke), *Passion Play* (Donmar Warehouse at The Comedy Theatre), *Dangerous Corner* (Palace Theatre, Watford), *Tess of the D'Urbervilles* (JFK Repertory Company) and *Death of an Elephant* (Orange Tree Theatre).

Television includes *The Mother, Ahead of the Class, The Bill, The Time Master* and *Silent Witness*.

Film includes *Mark of Cain, Vera Drake* (nominated for a BAFTA Award in 2005 for Actress in a Supporting Role), *All or Nothing, Topsy Turvy, Drinking Crude* and *Loop*.

Andrew French *Mathieu*

Andrew trained at the Webber Douglas Academy.

Theatre includes *Titus Andronicus* (The Project, Dublin), *As You Like It* (Wyndhams Theatre), *References to Salvador Dali Make Me Hot* (Young Vic / Arcola), *The Taming of the Shrew* (Nottingham Playhouse), *The Ramayana* (National Theatre / Birmingham Rep), *The Merchant of Venice, Troilus and Cressida, The Darker Face of the Earth* (National Theatre), *The Taming of the Shrew* (English Touring Theatre), *The Merchant of Venice, The Honest Whore* (Shakespeare's Globe), *Epitaph For The Whales* (Gate Theatre), *Things Fall Apart* (Royal Court Theatre), *The Tempest* (Shared Experience tour), *The Tempest* (Theatr Clwyd / Nottingham Playhouse), *Ebb Tide* (Citizens' Theatre, Glasgow), *Othello* (Oxford Shakespeare Festival), *Measure for Measure* (Shakespeare Institution), *The Tempest* (Harvard University).

Television includes *Perfect Parents, Primeval, Soundproof, Holby City, The Bill, Doctors, Trust, A Touch of Frost, Family Affairs, Casualty, Burnside* and *Tough Love*.

Film includes *Exorcist: In the Beginning, Exorcist: Dominion, Beyond Borders, The Merchant of Venice, Boxed In* and *Let's Stick Together*.

Jade Williams *Freya*

Theatre includes *Little Voice* (Harrogate Theatre), *Market Boy* (National Theatre), *'Low Dat* (Birmingham Rep), *Dark Of The Moon* (Kings Head) and *Les Miserables* (Palace Theatre).

Television includes *EastEnders, Judge John Deed, The Canterbury Tales – The Pardoner's Tale, Doctors, Serious and Organised, William and Mary, The Bill, Mile High, Being April, Lloyd and Hill, Casualty, Other People's Children, The Sins, Hope and Glory, Bad Girls, Paddington Bear, Anything's Possible, Grange Hill, Wavelength, Plotlands* and *Black Hearts in Battersea*.

Film includes *Anne Frank, Ghost Story* and *Love 'N' Lyrics*.

Radio includes *Secrets, Westway, Songs that Houses Sing, Up and Down in Silverton* and *A Handful of Dust*.

Georgia Fitch *Writer*

Georgia was joint Sheila Lemon writer in residence at The Bush Theatre in 2001. Her first play for The Bush was the highly acclaimed *adrenalin…heart*, performed in 2002 and again in 2004, and which transferred to the Tokyo International Theatre Festival. Other work includes *Madonna and Child* (Royal Court rehearsed reading) and *Arrivals* (Old Red Lion). Together with Tracy O'Flaherty, she co-wrote the plays *The Footballer's Wife* (Riverside Studios) and *Come Dancing* (Old Red Lion). Georgia was writer on attachment at Soho Theatre in 2005–6, and writer in residence at BBC Radio Drama in 2004. Radio includes *Romeo and Juliet in Southwark, I Met a Boy, With Sweetness, Fortune's Always Hiding* and *adrenalin…heart*. Georgia has developed television work for Carlton and the BBC, and is currently under commission to Soho Theatre, BBC World Service and Radio 4.

Mike Bradwell *Director*

Mike Bradwell has been Artistic Director of The Bush Theatre for ten years, and associated with the theatre since 1974. He has directed over 40 plays for The Bush, and *I Like Mine With A Kiss* marks his last play as Artistic Director. He appeared in Mike Leigh's *Bleak Moments*, was an actor / musician with The Ken Campbell Road Show, and an underwater escapologist with Hirst's Carivari. Mike founded Hull Truck Theatre Company in 1971 and directed all their shows for ten years, including several of his own plays.

Directing work for The Bush Theatre includes *Love and Understanding* by Joe Penhall (also at The Long Wharf Theatre, USA), *Love You, Too* by Doug Lucie, *Dead Sheep*, *Little Baby Nothing* and *Shang-a-Lang* by Catherine Johnson (also 1999 national tour), *Howie the Rookie* by Mark O'Rowe (also 1999 Edinburgh Festival and internationally), *Resident Alien* by Tim Fountain (also New York Theater Workshop), *Blackbird* by Adam Rapp, *Airsick* by Emma Frost, *adrenalin…heart* by Georgia Fitch (also Tram Theatre, Tokyo), *Gong Donkeys* and *The Glee Club* by Richard Cameron (also at The Duchess Theatre, the Bolton Octagon, Galway Arts Festival and on tour), *The Girl with Red Hair* by Sharman MacDonald (Edinburgh Lyceum and Hampstead Theatre), *When You Cure Me* by Jack Thorne, *crooked* by Catherine Trieschmann and *Pumpgirl* by Abbie Spallen.

Mike has directed for other theatres including Hampstead Theatre, Tricycle Theatre, The King's Head, West Yorkshire Playhouse, The National Theatre of Brent and The Royal Court, where he was Associate Director.

Mike has also written and directed extensively for TV and Radio, including the BBC film *Happy Feet*.

Libby Watson *Designer*

Previous work for The Bush includes *crooked* by Catherine Trieschmann, directed by Mike Bradwell.

Current work includes *The War Next Door* by Tamsin Ogelsby (Tricycle Theatre), *Aladdin* (Bury Theatre Royal Big Tent), *The French Lieutenant's Woman* (tour), *Blonde Bombshells of 1943* (Bolton / Hampstead / 2007 tour) and *Macbeth* (Bristol Old Vic Studio). Recent work includes *Three Sisters* (Cryptic Theatre Tour / Hackney Empire), *Gem of the Ocean* by August Wilson (Tricycle Theatre), *What's in the Cat* by Linda Brogan (Manchester Contact Theatre / Royal Court Upstairs), *High Heel Parrotfish* (Theatre Royal Stratford East), *Opera Showcase* (London Opera Studio / Hackney Empire), *Deranged Marriage*, written and directed by Pravesh Kumar (tour), *Rifco* (Warwick Arts Centre / Theatre Royal Stratford East / Windsor Theatre Royal), *I Dreamt I Dwelt in Marble Halls*, *Garden of Llangoed* and *Comedians* (Watermill Theatre, Newbury).

James Farncombe

Lighting Designer

Previously at the Bush: *crooked.*

Credits include: *Three Sisters* and *Forward* (Birmingham Rep); *Blonde Bombshells of 1943*, *Nathan the Wise*, *Osama the Hero*, *A Single Act* and *The Maths Tutor* (Hampstead Theatre, London); *Blest Be the Tie* and *What's in the Cat* (Royal Court, London); *Improbable Fiction* (directed by Alan Ayckbourn), *Making Waves* and *Soap* (Stephen Joseph Theatre, Scarborough); *Blues for Mr Charlie* (Tricycle and Ipswich Wolsey); *A Funny Thing Happened on the Way to the Forum* and *Vincent in Brixton* (New Wolsey, Ipswich); *Beautiful Thing* (Nottingham Playhouse); *Dead Funny* and *Abigail's Party* (York Theatre Royal); *Sing Yer Heart Out for the Lads*, *Lord of the Flies*, *The Twits* and *Bloodtide* (Pilot Theatre Company); *Accidental Death of an Anarchist*, *A View from the Bridge*, *What the Butler Saw*, *The Hypochondriac* (nominated *Manchester Evening News* Awards Best Design Team 2003), *Dead Funny*, *Popcorn* and *Improbable Fiction* (The Octagon, Bolton); *To Kill a Mockingbird*, *Master Harold and the Boys*, *West Side Story*, *Death of a Salesman*, *Peter Pan*, *The Witches*, *Plague of Innocence* and *Unsuitable Girls* (Leicester Haymarket Theatre); *High Heel Parrotfish*, *Urban Afro Saxons* and *Funny Black Women on the Edge* (Theatre Royal, Stratford East); *Playboy of the West Indies* (Tricycle and Nottingham Playhouse); *This Lime Tree Bower* (The Belgrade Coventry); *Hysteria* (Exeter Northcott); *Amy's View* (Salisbury Playhouse and Royal Theatre, Northampton); *Krapp's Last Tape* (Lakeside Arts, Nottingham); *Hang Lenny Pope*, *Street Trilogy* and *Cloudburst* (Theatre Absolute); *The Blue Room* and *The Elephant Man* (Worcester Swan Theatre); *East Is East* and *A Woman of No Importance* (New Vic Theatre, Stoke); *Goldilocks* (Lyric Theatre, Hammersmith); *Private Fears in Public Places*, *Speed-the-Plow*, *A Day in the Death of Joe Egg*, *The Price* and *Larkin with Women* (Manchester Library Theatre).

David Benke *Sound Designer*

Music and sound design for theatre / opera / film / radio and dance. Recent work includes *The Invention of Life* (Vienna Festival), *Macbeth* (Staatstheatre, Stuttgart), *Salome* (Schauspiel Frankfurt) and *Dangerous Liaisons* (Theater am Neumarkt, Zurich).

Nadia Latif *Assistant Director*

Originally from Sudan, Nadia graduated from UCL in 2006 with a BA in English. She is co-founder and Artistic Director of Tabula Rasa Theatre, a company dedicated to the production of new writing and working with young, multi-ethnic actors, writers and directors. She is a veteran of the Edinburgh Fringe Festival, and is currently training as a director at RADA. Directing credits include: *The Importance of Being Turbann'd*, *Othello*, *Kindertransport*, *The Lying Kind*, *A Midsummer Night's Dream*, *Look After Lulu*, *Our Country's Good*, *Six Degrees of Separation* and *Waiting for Godot.*

The Bush Theatre

The Bush Theatre is one of the most celebrated new writing theatres
in the world. We have an international reputation for discovering,
nurturing and producing the best new theatre writers from the
widest range of backgrounds, and for presenting their work to the
highest possible standards. We look for exciting new voices that
tell contemporary stories with wit, style and passion and we champion work that is both
provocative and entertaining.

With around 40,000 people enjoying our productions each year, The Bush has produced
hundreds of ground-breaking premieres since its inception 35 years ago. The theatre produces
up to eight productions of new plays a year, many of them Bush commissions, and hosts guest
productions by leading companies and artists from all over the world.

The Bush is widely acclaimed as the seedbed for the best new playwrights, many of whom
have gone on to become established names in the entertainment industry, including Steve
Thompson, Jack Thorne, Amelia Bullmore, Dennis Kelly, Chloë Moss, David Eldridge, Stephen
Poliakoff, Snoo Wilson, Terry Johnson, Kevin Elyot, Doug Lucie, Dusty Hughes, Sharman
Macdonald, Billy Roche, Catherine Johnson, Philip Ridley, Richard Cameron, Jonathan Harvey,
Conor McPherson, Joe Penhall, Helen Blakeman, Mark O'Rowe and Charlotte Jones. We
also champion the introduction of new talent to the industry, whilst continuing to attract
major acting and directing talents, including Richard Wilson, Nadim Sawalha, Bob Hoskins,
Alan Rickman, Antony Sher, Stephen Rea, Frances Barber, Lindsay Duncan, Brian Cox, Kate
Beckinsale, Patricia Hodge, Simon Callow, Alison Steadman, Jim Broadbent, Tim Roth, Jane
Horrocks, Mike Leigh, Mike Figgis, Mike Newell, Victoria Wood and Julie Walters.

The Bush has won over one hundred awards, and developed an enviable reputation for touring
its acclaimed productions nationally and internationally. Recent tours and transfers include
the West End transfer of *Whipping It Up* and international tour of *Pumpgirl* (2007), a national
number one tour of *Mammals* (2006), an international tour of *After The End* (2005–6),
adrenalin...heart representing the UK in the Tokyo International Arts Festival (2004), the West
End transfer (2002) and national tour of *The Glee Club* (2004), a European tour of *Stitching*
(2003) and Off-Broadway transfers of *Howie the Rookie* and *Resident Alien*. Film adaptations
include *Beautiful Thing* and *Disco Pigs*.

The Bush Theatre provides a free script reading service, receiving over 1000 scripts through
the post every year, and reading them all. This is one small part of a comprehensive
Writers' Development Programme, which includes workshops, one-to-one dramaturgy,
rehearsed readings, research bursaries, masterclasses, residencies and commissions. We have
also launched a pilot scheme for an ambitious new education, training and professional
development programme, **bushfutures**, providing opportunities for different sectors of the
community and professionals to access the expertise of Bush writers, directors, designers,
technicians and actors, and to play an active role in influencing the future development of the
theatre and its programme.

The Bush Theatre is extremely proud of its reputation for artistic excellence, its friendly
atmosphere, and its undisputed role as a major force in shaping the future of British theatre.

At The Bush Theatre

Executive Producer	**Fiona Clark**
General Manager	**Angela Bond**
Literary Manager	**Abigail Gonda**
Finance Manager	**Dave Smith**
Production Manager	**Robert Holmes**
Marketing Manager	**Nicki Marsh**
Development Manager	**Sophie Hussey**
Resident Stage Manager	**Ros Terry**
Assistant General Manager	**Sarah McEwen**
Literary Assistant	**Jane Fallowfield**
Box Office Supervisor	**Darren Elliott**
Box Office Assistants	**Charlotte Ive, Catherine Nix-Collins**
Front of House Duty Managers	**Kellie Batchelor, Adrian Christopher, Abigail Lunb, Glenn Mortimer, Kirstin Smith, Lois Tucker**
Duty Technicians	**Jason Kirk, Esteban Nunez, Tom White**
Associate Artists	**Tanya Burns, Es Devlin, Richard Jordan, Paul Miller**
Press Representative	**Alex Gammie** 020 7837 8333
Pearson Writer in Residence	**Jack Thorne**

The Bush Theatre
Shepherds Bush Green
London W12 8QD
Box Office: 020 7610 4224
www.bushtheatre.co.uk

The Alternative Theatre Company Ltd. (The Bush Theatre)
is a Registered Charity number: 270080
Co. registration number 1221968
VAT no. 228 3168 73

Be there at the beginning...

... and help discover the gems of tomorrow

We are most grateful to the following Patron members, charitable trusts and companies for their support and gifts in-kind. This support has doubled in the last year and directly enables us to provide the **Writers' Development Programme** of one-to-one dramaturgy, workshops and bursaries and to launch **bushfutures**, our new education, training and professional development programme.

Join as a Patron member today and help us to grow tomorrow's talent. In return you will enjoy complimentary tickets, signed playtexts, special events...and a warm feeling inside.

For a Patron pack or information on supporting our programmes, please call 020 7602 3703, email development@bushtheatre.co.uk or visit www.bushtheatre.co.uk

Current supporters

The Bush Theatre gratefully acknowledges the valuable support of Arts Council, England and the London Borough of Hammersmith & Fulham.

Lone Star
Princess of Darkness

Handful of Stars
Gianni Alen-Buckley
Joe Hemani

Glee Club
Anonymous
Jim Broadbent
Clyde Cooper
Adam Kenwright
Curtis Brown Group Ltd
Richard & Elizabeth Philipps
Alan Rickman
John & Tita Shakeshaft

Beautiful Thing
Anonymous
Alan Brodie
Kate Brooke
David Brooks
Clive Butler
Matthew Byam Shaw
Jeremy Conway
Anna Donald
Mike Figgis
Vivien Goodwin
Sheila Hancock
David Hare
Lucy Heller
Bill Keeling
Laurie Marsh
Michael McCoy
Tim McInnerny & Annie Gosney

John Michie
John & Jacqui Pearson
Mr & Mrs A Radcliffe
Wendy Rawson
John Reynolds
David Pugh & Dafydd Rogers
Barry Serjent
Brian D Smith
Barrie & Roxanne Wilson

Rookies
Anonymous
Neil Adleman
Ross Anderson
Pauline Asper
Constance Byam Shaw
Geraldine Caufield
Nigel Clark
Nina Drucker
Sian Hansen
Mr G Hopkinson
Joyce Hytner, ACT IV
Robert Israel for Gordon & Co.
Peter James
Hardeep Kalsi
Casarotto Ramsay & Associates Ltd
Robin Kermode
Ray Miles
Mr & Mrs Malcolm Ogden
Radfin
Clare Rich
Mark Roberts
David Robinson

Tracey Scoffield
Councillor Minnie Scott Russell
Martin Shenfield
Loveday Waymouth
Clare Williams
Alison Winter

Platinum Corporate members
Anonymous

Silver
The Agency (London) Ltd

Bronze
Anonymous
Act Productions Ltd
The Peters, Fraser & Dunlop Group Ltd

Trust and Foundation Supporters
The Earls Court and Olympia Charitable Trust
Garfield Weston Foundation
The John Thaw Foundation
The Kobler Trust
The Martin Bowley Charitable Trust
The Mercers' Company
The Royal Victoria Hall Charitable Trust
The Thistle Trust
The Vandervell Foundation

Business Support
Marks & Spencer
Pol Roger Ltd

What a gem!   **thebushtheatre**

Spring/Summer Season

The Bush Theatre presents The Citizens' Theatre production of

TOM FOOL
by Franz Xaver Kroetz | directed by Clare Lizzimore
28 March – 21 April
'Superb, powerful…and unforgettable' ***** *The Scotsman*

The Bush Theatre, by arrangement with Trademark, ATG and Finola Dwyer, presents

ELLING
adapted by Simon Bent | directed by Paul Miller
25 April – 26 May
John Simm stars in a new adaptation of the award-winning cult film

Third Stage and Amy Kassai Ltd in association with The Bush Theatre
present the world premiere of a new English version of

TRANCE
written and directed by Shoji Kokami
6 – 30 June
A mind-bending and hilarious tale of friendship, insanity and identity

And currently in the West End…

Act Productions, Ambassador Theatre Group, Bush Productions, Matthew Byam Shaw,
Mark Goucher and Wimpole Theatre present The Bush Theatre production of

WHIPPING IT UP
by Steve Thompson
directed by Tamara Harvey, original direction by Terry Johnson
with Robert Bathurst, Kellie Bright, Lee Ross, Nicholas Rowe,
Helen Schlesinger and Richard Wilson
New Ambassadors Theatre, from 22 February

Booking: 0870 534 4444 | www.ticketmaster.co.uk

www.bushtheatre.co.uk | 020 7610 4224

b

Georgia Fitch

I LIKE MINE WITH A KISS

First published in 2007 by Oberon Books Ltd.
521 Caledonian Road, London N7 9RH
Tel: 020 7607 3637 / Fax: 020 7607 3629
e-mail: info@oberonbooks.com
www.oberonbooks.com

A catalogue record for this book is available from the British Library.

ISBN: 1 84002 724 X / 978-1-84002-724-2

Cover image by istockphoto

Printed in Great Britain by Antony Rowe Ltd, Chippenham.

Characters

LOUISE
39, a teacher in a London comprehensive

ANNIE
39, a single mother

JIM
39, independent film maker / artist

JEAN
65, mother to Annie and grandmother to Freya

FREYA
16 and studying, daughter to Annie

MATHIEU
33, a working guy

The action takes place over one year, in various flats, bars and other locations in London.

Time: 2007.

Note on staging: Lou's and Annie's worlds should be seen simultaneously, blending in and out of one another over the course of the play. Flats double as bars; parks become the gates of Freya's school; each character's separate world connects with and spills into each of the others'.

Note on the text: a slash '/' indicates an interruption. Capitals denote emotional intensity rather than volume.

Myth *mith n.* a fable: a legend embodying primitive faith in the supernatural: an invented story: an imaginary person or thing, as in 'his fortune proved to be a myth'.

Love and thanks to
Mike Bradwell, Abigail Gonda and all at The Bush; Wendy Nottingham, Melissa Simmons and all of the actors who worked on this play in both the workshop and reading; especially Julia Ford and Nicola Wilson for the initial yes; and my premiership cast

In rememberance of Russell Mabey

for
Maureen and George Fitch

Act One

A party upstairs in a bar in central London. LOUISE is entertaining her guests with a pseudo-erotic dance, her usual comic and outrageous party routine. Loud, raw music plays: smoky, charged and somewhat seedy. LOUISE runs away and is followed by ANNIE. Both women are drunk. LOUISE's white dress has a huge red stain and her hair is ridiculously ruffled. Outside the ladies' toilet, downstairs.

LOU: He said have a baby babe /

ANNIE: What?

LOU: ...the bastard from before. He said have a baby babe. If you love me you will have my baby and I'll stop drinking. I will marry you and my baby: babe, my little boy...or girl...

ANNIE: I know you've told me...I know this story...I know...I know Lou I know...babe...why are we talking about /

LOU: He was vodka on the cornflakes: the bastard from before. It was yeah, a risk. I mean he didn't even have a bed and I said don't make this any more difficult than it already is. (*She demonstrates.*) He gets me at the door right? Stained thin breath and trying not to fall over, with his hands around my throat, he spits out /

ANNIE: Do you want a ciggie? Come on...come... (*She opens her arms.*) What have you spilt down your dress...look at you...look at you Lou /

LOU: Are you having a good time...a nice time...a...yeah give us a cuddle /

ANNIE attempts to cuddle LOUISE. LOUISE then moves away.

I can have work and love /

ANNIE: What?

LOU: Bastard /

ANNIE: From before…oh yeah…oh yeah…oh /

LOU: …fifty per cent of successful women are single I shout…
Off you go then, off you go darling Louise, but what is it
you do again? He screams in my face. Catch me while you
can, he goes, catch me whilst you…and I was squeezed up
tight in the corner and I couldn't breathe, I couldn't /

ANNIE exits.

ANNIE: (*Offstage.*) Every time you tell this tale /

*ANNIE returns with some paper towels from the toilet. ANNIE
attempts to mop LOUISE's dress.*

LOU: Do you want to have it all Louise?

ANNIE: This needs a good soak, not a lot I can /

LOU: I ran out that flat and I kept running man, and past many
many shiny bastards Annie, never turning back: never
giving them a second or a sniff. Shaking me, I am shaking,
shake when I'm drunk, drunk!

ANNIE: Never mind. (*Beat. Trying really hard with the dress.*)
Shall we go back to your party in a minute eh darling?

LOU: Fifteen per cent of women do not want kids I told this
new bastard upstairs and it's growing. There's a childless
revolution happening.

ANNIE: Fantastic!

LOU: He smiles, runs his tobacco fingers through his glossy
independent film maker hair and grins nice and wide.
(*Beat.*) Beautiful teeth.

ANNIE: Who?

LOU: Bastard from now! And I am back there Annie, after
all the strength searching and crystals. I am back there,
immediately giving it all away, on my birthday, and the
new bastard is winning and /

ANNIE: …what? (*She gives up on the dress.*)

LOU: (*She looks at ANNIE.*) …why my life is such a – (*She kicks the wall and screams. Big beat.*) Do you think I am aggressive?

ANNIE: …maybe…a bit oversensitive…a bit /

LOU: …why don't I have kids and a sorted home life and I can't answer that. I can't find anyone or…anything about this on-line…that doesn't make me sound like an earnest… I have been researching y'know /

ANNIE: Okay /

LOU: …a bit late at night and…my search engine screws me y'see, life has apparently screwed me and the new bastard wants to… (*She drunkenly whistles.*)

ANNIE: So why you kissing the new…bastard. I don't understand…I don't…I /

LOU: I shouted at him upstairs, did you hear, did you?

ANNIE: Yes…everyone did…even people in /

LOU: I said I don't want another lover. I had a lover, I HAD A LOVER, who hasn't turned up tonight, can you believe that Annie…can you? (*Big big beat.*) Why do I keep on remembering horrible horrible times?

ANNIE: Because you can't take your drink and you will never learn and I am sure Matt – YOUR…LOVER… UNDERCOVER…WHATEVER! – has a good excuse for not being here and /

LOU: Thought Matt would have come Annie, have left him messages, thought he could have made the effort and so it's finally the end…me and him, him and me and finally the /

ANNIE: …maybe something…he may have /

LOU: He eventually got me on the mobile: bastard from before /

ANNIE: Sorry /

LOU: Said he was going to kill himself /

ANNIE: They always say that /

LOU: Screaming at me down the phone, without children what
is a woman's identity, who are you anyway woman, who
are you? Shooting at the heart, no messing. I goes don't
need a little me running about to make me feel complete
and sixty per cent of the population is a mistake. (*Beat.*) I
am not in love with myself enough, that I have to or can
only love a clone.

ANNIE: (*Sighs.*)

LOU: That wasn't a dig at you /

ANNIE: Was it not?

LOU: Love you love /

ANNIE: (*Beat.*)

LOU: I came back with an argument up upstairs see. I met
him – matched him… Each individual must earn their
mortality…you get me?

ANNIE: You do, you always come back with a /

LOU: I said to him, Matt who hasn't turned up tonight, who
hasn't turned up tonight and who has children but he's not
here…and I have friends of my age who want children
so badly, yet it ain't happening because they are too…
However then my friend scraped a man off the internet
and within three months she's having a baby TA DAH…so
if I really wanted one? Then there are other friends doing
all the two point four and they are dead from the waist
and /

ANNIE: Was he enjoying this conversation: him upstairs…new
bastard?

LOU: (*Lost to herself, remembering.*) CATCH ME WHILE
YOU CAN. CATCH ME WHILE YOU CAN…HE
UPSTAIRS LAUGHS, MATT: UNDERCOVER MUST

BE LAUGHING, HAVING A GOOD TIME AND
LAUGHING AND ARE THEY ALL LAUGHING, ALL
LAUGHING AT US? /

ANNIE: Now you've really lost me…now you really are…

Silence. LOUISE looks at ANNIE and smiles. ANNIE goes to her friend and kisses her.

I might let Peter come home with me.

LOU: Freya's at yer mum's.

ANNIE: Shall we go back?

LOU: People do look at you y'know: people look at your… purpose.

ANNIE:

LOU: On a Sunday afternoon, no kids, walking around the park, you appear to have nothing /

ANNIE:

LOU: …see it in people's eyes /

ANNIE: Nobody really wants to talk to me tonight…now who might it be in my best interests to converse with /

LOU: Most people still opt for family…it's easy: it sort of works…

ANNIE gives LOUISE a look.

Bastard from now speak /

ANNIE: Having been a mum for the last sixteen years, I'll tell him thanks for that /

LOUISE sits on a chair, starts to cry: drunken sobs.

LOU: HE UPSTAIRS IS /

ANNIE: Okay so you've got it on with a man upstairs…
DON'T BEAT YOURSELF UP…you are becoming /

LOU:

ANNIE: …you always advocated…making it up as you went along /

LOU:

ANNIE: Well at least you won't be sleeping with him…Jim… that's his name isn't it…him upstairs…the…bastard from now /

LOU: Bastard from before started seeing someone else a week later, they have two sons now…twins…TWINNIES…end of /

She falls off the chair, her skirt is hanging off her and we can see her underwear. ANNIE goes to help her up.

ANNIE: Peter will never know what he wants.

LOU: Do you still love me?

JIM enters.

JIM: So that's where you are…causing havoc down here /

LOU: What you going to do about it then?

ANNIE exits. LOUISE and JIM alone.

DANGEROUS…well so I've been told.

JIM: I've got to get up at five…

LOU: …schemes of work…Year Ten! (*Beat. She turns and stares at him.*) Well we had better…

JIM: Better?

LOU: Go now then /

JIM: Right /

LOU: Right /

JIM: How do you like your eggs love?

LOU:

JIM: Scrambled?

LOU:

JIM: Poached? Come on babe /

LOU: In between two slices of buttered white, lots of salt, fried and dripping of course…and as I bite in, and as I bite in, it dribbles down my chin and you…and you /

JIM: What?

LOU: You lick it off and you fuck me, you fuck me /

JIM: Okay…okay!

Blends to ANNIE's flat. JEAN enters with FREYA, who immediately exits.

JEAN: There's nowhere to park. Daddy's been driving around for hours. So was it a good party? What was it like?

ANNIE: What's wrong with Freya mum?

JEAN: Said she had to check her messages, there's someone at school, she er…a girl at school, talk to her, you talk to her, when you talk to your daughter /

ANNIE: What?

JEAN: Any man of your dreams there?

ANNIE: Peter came.

JEAN: Oh well as long as you all enjoyed yourself.

ANNIE: You don't look well mum /

JEAN: Your brothers send their love and both apologise for not being able to come to the do and /

ANNIE: I know families, their families mum.

JEAN: Look I have to go and /

ANNIE: You could risk it y'know…there won't be any parking attendants around now…anyway it's a Sunday. Phone dad on the mobile and get him to come on up…please?

JEAN: He doesn't know how to answer his new phone, I have to help him with that, with all things technical…we won't get him babe /

ANNIE:

JEAN: No we had better shoot off, going up the golf club.

ANNIE: Shall I put the kettle on eh?

JEAN: Midget man…that little midget man, I told you about, with the fantastic voice, does all the Sinatra classics. He packs them in, meeting people. Should be a good one… should be a…

ANNIE:

JEAN: Your father had a bit of road rage coming here, silly old silly sod /

ANNIE: One of these days /

JEAN: I know darling, I know.

ANNIE: Oh mum, mummy, give us a cuddle please?

JEAN hugs her daughter. ANNIE looks at her mum.

JEAN: Have you been…?

JEAN looks at her daughter.

ANNIE: Do you feel alright mum?

JEAN: I am fine babe, I am…

JEAN kisses her daughter and laughs. ANNIE shouts off to FREYA.

ANNIE: Come and say goodbye to grandma. Freya come and say thank you and goodbye to /

FREYA enters and gives a big kiss to her grandma.

JEAN: Come and say bye to yer nan.

FREYA: Can I come and stay again soon?

JEAN: Of course…we will be up soon too lovely.

FREYA: Love you.

JEAN: Here's a bag of shopping, supermarket doing some cheap deals…so got you some things and they had a sale at…couple of pairs of knickers and that sort of stuff. Always come in handy knickers…and er…I got to go babe…I've got to /

JEAN exits, FREYA still in her coat.

ANNIE: Aren't you hot?

FREYA: In a minute mum…in a…has anyone called for me? I want to check my messages…just starting the computer /

ANNIE: Let me give you a kiss, let me…come here…come here /

ANNIE kisses her daughter.

FREYA: I'm exhausted, so tired…I have to check my messages mum /

ANNIE pulls her closer. FREYA breaks away.

Just watched telly last night… I wanted to. Trash on the plasma. Grandma let me use her phone. I voted sixteen times for /

ANNIE: They haven't got any money…don't be fooled Freya, don't be fooled.

FREYA: Grandma gave me twenty pounds, but she told me not to tell you /

ANNIE: Greedy…

FREYA: She insisted mum and steak and chips. (*Beat.*) A portion big enough for three.

FREYA laughs.

ANNIE: That's how they communicate their love.

FREYA: Did you and Lou both pull at the party?

ANNIE: We behaved ourselves /

FREYA: Bet Lou got drunk and cried and lap danced and showed her delicious…arse and yer self?

ANNIE: Go and have a bath /

FREYA: I don't want one /

ANNIE: Course work after /

FREYA: I've just got through the /

ANNIE: Come on…come on /

FREYA: You seem /

ANNIE: I'm a bit tired that's all /

FREYA: A bit hung over…a bit I don't know tense and /

ANNIE: Okay…go and run a bath or shall I do it for you?

FREYA goes into bathroom, returns with sweatshirt.

FREYA: Mum who does this belong to?

FREYA tries it on.

ANNIE: Someone left it at the party…brought it back…will ring round… Lou liked the present you chose for her /

FREYA: She knows how to dress…

ANNIE: …hungry?

FREYA: Grandma was saying to grandad about all of your friends being single. Some men must be out there

– grandma said…grandad said it was because they didn't want to be bored /

ANNIE:

FREYA: Women!

ANNIE: Grandad said that?

FREYA: I said it was because they had sense, yet they were too scared to love another woman…they didn't have the courage…the courage to be…and lick /

Did Peter turn up?

ANNIE: …and why you ask?

FREYA: …is he still with his new girlfriend: minger?

ANNIE: They split up /

FREYA: Prozac Pete, charisma bypass /

ANNIE: There's a programme I want to watch on the television /

FREYA: I told Grandma, I like this girl at sixth form; it was a kind of crush. Not overtly sexual, but fulfilling and /

ANNIE: What?

FREYA: She said she didn't think she could give me any advice, said I should talk to you. I am going to check my messages and I don't want a bath. I know you said I could have come to the party, but now I am glad I didn't, yeah…glad I didn't…mum…mummy…mother.

The doorbell. LOUISE enters flustered, she kisses the exiting FREYA.

LOU: Have been trying you all day /

Nods to a departing FREYA.

ANNIE: Are you alright?

LOU: Peter?

ANNIE: Well nobody else there /

LOU: I had to get the morning after, hate doing that, condom came off. Quizzed by a woman in hijab, thought she wasn't going give it to me. Then efficiently passed over to what appeared to be her pharmacist husband…hurrah. A wave of early religious guilt shot right through me, so I soon put a stop to all that. I thought they were going to announce it over the tannoy, Slag in Boots, come see Slag in Boots /

ANNIE: I had to get it too.

LOU: Never worth it eh?

ANNIE: I have actually…never taken it before /

Beat.

LOU: Well if you're sick you have to take it again /

ANNIE: Did the bastard from now: did Jim…did he live up to your expectations?

LOU: Well out of ten…I definitely gave him…one. (*Beat.*) We are a shoddy pair of /

ANNIE: Speak for yourself /

LOU: I have got to clean up my act, I really have…I really /

FREYA enters and stares at her mother.

ANNIE: (*To LOU.*) Look do you want a lift home…fancy a movie tomorrow?

LOU: Taking sixth form to theatre /

FREYA: Peter: toothbrush was out /

ANNIE:

FREYA: I am going to have an early night. Her name is Lucy. The girl at sixth form, her name is Lucy. Thank you for asking mum…thank you for being interested in /

ANNIE: Freya, Freya!

FREYA exits.

LOU: I am quite good with teenagers.

LOUISE follows FREYA into her bedroom. ANNIE takes the pill packet out of her handbag, she looks at it, she stares into space. She puts the pill packet back into her bag. She goes to placate her daughter.

ANNIE: (*Exiting.*) Freya…when's your first lecture? Freya… Freya, Louise, Louise!

Music plays. LOUISE alone. MATHIEU enters another bar in North London. ANNIE should be seen in the background. FREYA should come in, and then leave again, leaving ANNIE alone. LOUISE kisses MATHIEU and unwraps a present. He watches her with intensity.

MATT: You look nice, you look gorgeous…

LOU: You think all women are /

MATT: I got a few of your messages: why didn't you come to my party? You are a cunt texts.

LOU: I was drunk and upset.

LOUISE gets to the present, a football calendar and some perfume.

MATT: Woman in the shop said that, this is a new make and it's only a joke…the calendar only a joke, it's for er …yeah?

LOU: I can't be angry with you, I can never be…really angry with…

She turns the page over to a footballer, who he resembles, puts it next to his face.

MATT: If only man, if only.

She pulls him to her, kisses his cheek, then looks him in the eye. He plays with his phone again. Puts it to one side, rubs his legs and sighs.

LOU: You should of /

MATT: Can't be doing with…some of those people man /

LOU: I know me me me types /

MATT: I'm just a normal guy…I can't be doing with them people, you know me /

LOU: And you know me…I was deeply hurt.

Silence. He moves into her.

MATT: …you smell amazing man: real real amazing…scent of a woman…

Long long silence. He fidgets.

LOU: Charm me then…

MATT: Love it when you are edgy man: that fire in a woman /

LOU: You are /

MATT: I have really got to make a call, it's about my er… children.

LOU: Okay.

MATT: No, it's alright, I'll wait. I'll wait, I'll…

More silence.

LOU: How's work?

MATT: Busy…yeah /

Silence. LOUISE wipes her nose and he watches her.

LOU: How's yer mum?

MATT: She's still in hospital.

LOU: Right.

MATT: Me and the boys went out at the weekend: wicked night down /

LOU: Kwarme tried it on with everyone, Andy fell asleep in the corner and you…

MATT: People were asking how you were and where you were /

LOU: Look I am trying really hard to be angry with you and /

He looks back at the calendar.

MATT: Never premiership enough though?

She sighs. He lights up, offers her a cigarette.

LOU: You look sexy when you smoke.

MATT: Only when I smoke?

LOU: I keep on bursting into tears see…when I think about us. Heading to forty and I think there comes a time when you have to sort of grow up.

MATT: Two kids, separated and but eh…

LOU: And I do love you…I care so much for you and you know I am a loyal person…it's just I don't like…lying?

MATT: (*Still playing with his phone.*) Don't bring things like that up please, don't start confusing, no heavy stuff, just relax yourself…look let me get you a drink and you relax yourself: you relax yourself /

She pulls him down and gets hold of his hand.

LOU: You didn't come /

MATT: Lots of guys chatting you up at the party, your eyes catching the room, who's there, what's /

LOU: Doesn't mean I really want it.

MATT: It's a bad time for me y'know…a bad time /

LOU: How are the girls...your children?

MATT: She's taking them down under. She told me on Saturday. I was preparing to come to the party with the boys, and then she told me. Felt all over the place man... confidence crashed and /

LOU: Has a date been set?

MATT: Need a stiff drink man /

LOU: What do you want? I'll get it...NO I WILL /

MATHIEU on his own, checking his phone. LOUISE returns with drinks.

MATT: MY CHILDREN, MY CHILDREN, MY GIRLS /

LOU: YOUR LOVE FOR THEM AND THEIR LOVE FOR YOU WON'T GO AWAY: THEY ADORE YOU: YOU KNOW THAT: YOU KNOW THAT /

MATT: This is too heavy man...too too deep.

LOU: ...what is the solicitor saying /

MATT: I can't /

LOU: I want to help you with this /

MATT: If she can prove that she can provide a good home: schooling, a better life in Australia there's nothing I can, she's got a real good chance of winning. She's their mother man, she is my children's mother, and she gets the say, sweet as. She's been planning it for a while man, nothing new man, nothing...well apart from getting a caped crusader suit and chaining myself to /

LOU: Have you sat down and spoke about it all to her?

MATT: Her new spectacled partner always comes to the door /

LOU: ...come here...

MATT: So come on tell me the juicy bits, the events from the party.

LOU: You should have come: regardless of your kids this... terrible situation, you can't keep hiding away, be my match man, step up man, who cares what you are supposed to be, what you think you should be, sod the...learned few, sod it all...step up and take your life...I kept on telling you, to take it man, take it, take what you deserve. I er got together...with someone on my birthday. I said I always would tell you... I know we haven't seen each other... naked y'know for a while. (*Beat.*) Have always been faithful in our mad set-up, you deserve my honesty, I will always be your friend...but I needed...I needed to feel /

MATT: Nah man, nah /

He stands up to leave. LOUISE physically pleads with him. He aggressively pushes her away.

I don't trust women man...I always said I don't trust women, got played out too many times man...too many, many /

LOU: Shall I go? Where does this leave us...?

Silence.

Respond to me come on...come on...

MATT:

LOU: Can I make you a cup of tea at home and we can...

MATT:

LOU: Sugar...undercover?

MATHIEU exits. Blends to ANNIE's flat. Time passes. ANNIE is being very domestic.

ANNIE: Lucy's family is absolutely amazing and Lucy's mother is a goddess. Freya just loves it over there, the food, the conversation and the family. Every night this week, I can't stop her, she is off. Lucy's dad is an actor, originally from the north but Freya says that you wouldn't know that from his accent and her mother writes...perfect. Mother is a size eight, despite the kids, she is a size eight and beautiful, porcelain posh. Their house is worth millions, on the hill, where primroses supposedly grow and three other siblings...children all at state schools, 'cause daddy was a socialist, although they have extra tutoring at home and a dog...two cats, house in France...a nanny called Latvia... come on how can I compete with that, tell me how can I possibly be /

LOUISE immediately lights up another cigarette.

LOU: ...the big argument then /

LOUISE exits.

ANNIE: The porcelain posh goddess has been asking Freya about her dad. Holding and stroking my daughter's hand and asking her about her dad...can you believe that? (*Beat.*) Isn't Freya cross that she never knew him, doesn't Freya feel cheated, POWERLESS?

LOUISE returns with a bottle of ANNIE's wine.

...if she wants to open up the goddess will listen... Thus the huge, I told you Freya your dad didn't want me...it was to do with me...and you could try and trace him if you wanted, we could look into it again...but you never wanted to did you...after he didn't reply to your two letters...then we both just started shouting and it got into a loud and full-scale /

LOU: I am pregnant /

ANNIE: What?

LOU: Bought a test from a shop. Positive. Did two more... positive.

ANNIE: Oh God /

LOU: I made a few calls. Saw my GP and she was okay. Distant doctor, but okay. She confirmed it. Pregnant. With …having a…up the duff babe!

She takes a drink, ANNIE goes to her.

I know I shouldn't be drinking. I should be keeping a clear head, but…I feel very weird…say something Annie /

ANNIE: Why didn't you tell me /

ANNIE has her arm around LOUISE.

LOU: My eggs must be screaming for it… they say as you get older your fertility drops, nonsense nonsense, just another plot to make us…conceive /

ANNIE: Let's be sensible about this now /

LOU: I hate being a bastard woman /

ANNIE: Are you sure the test was right?

LOU: My doctor confirmed it…it didn't work okay?

ANNIE: So the next step /

LOU: Yours worked…but me, no me and /

ANNIE:

LOUISE downs one drink, pours another.

LOU: I know this is the last bus now isn't it…the last bus. The night bus, and my only chance to get on it…jump on now eh…jump jump on /

ANNIE: Where you going?

LOU: To motherhood, being a mum, mummy land? The first bus comes along, when I was sorry fifteen and I didn't want to get on that. They would have had to frogmarch me onto that one. Some girls did, girls in my class, those whose lives were already over, written over and written off.

I knew there was something else, there must be something else. (*Beat.*) Then it's a wait until your early thirties /

ANNIE: Shall we have a coffee?

LOU: ...and your middle-class friends are all jumping on then, but being you have spent your life scraping yourself out of some proletariat poverty and now not having a baby is so boldly a class issue and because you want to keep up work-wise with your middle-class sisters, keep up, keep up, you avoid that bus too.

LOUISE pours ANNIE a drink, ANNIE goes to take it, then thinks twice.

So at last the night bus, and you are somehow in the queue. Nothing else is going in that direction... The bus then approaches and it stops, collecting up those along the way who want it, really want it and those for who alternatives have truly escaped them... (*Giving up. Beat.*) I need my two signatures and then it's... I am only seven weeks, can do the pills thing, I have the appointment next week...private, I am going private now...so come say something say /

ANNIE: I obviously know about these things /

LOU: You said your mother sorted out your...you didn't have to do a /

ANNIE: I was seventeen okay /

LOU: Is it still in your dreams?

ANNIE: What?

LOU: Is it still in your dreams come on?

Silence. ANNIE sits watching LOUISE.

...some hardcore sight in the States...targeted for teens. It warned that I would basically never emotionally recover and subsequently be damned by the Lord... It would always be in my dreams /

ANNIE: You don't have to approach everything with such /

LOU: (*Beat.*) I've checked it all out!

ANNIE: The party was such a bad idea…loads of stress and then this /

LOU: We did what we had to do /

ANNIE: Both were appallingly drunk.

Silence.

I have to go and pick up Freya soon.

LOU: She's sixteen, she comes home on her own.

ANNIE: I feel I need to…

LOU: The Madonna?

ANNIE: …she also said that I was crowding her, not allowing her to breathe, I map my life through her, it was all hurtful stuff, I had it in my head to meet her from school and take her out somewhere…classy /

LOU: Do you think I should sue…would I get anywhere?

ANNIE: No.

LOU: I did in a moment of madness…think about having it: dupe Matt into believing it was his /

ANNIE: Matt?

LOU: We come from the same place and that means everything to me…now /

ANNIE: Look Freya, I'd rather we didn't talk about it…in front of her and /

LOU: This isn't all a criticism of you /

ANNIE: What bus did I get on then…it didn't seem to get a mention, in your summing…

Silence.

LOU: I want my mum…I want my mum…horrible horrible world…I want a mum…

ANNIE goes to her and cuddles her.

ANNIE: I'll be your mum…I might be good at it, although not doing very well at the moment with my own daughter /

She strokes LOUISE's hair.

LOU: Will you…will you?

ANNIE: Yeah I will…of course I…will. Everything is going to be alright mate /

LOUISE moves away from ANNIE.

LOU: He is going to have to give me some money…the bastard from now. I am going to make him… Hasn't answered any of my calls…but he will…he will and after trying to be so sex in the…

ANNIE: It's television.

LOU:

ANNIE: So when you meet…Jim…do you want me to come with? I mean I could wait in the car or something or is that a really bad idea?

LOU: God I know those sort of men…

ANNIE: …obviously /

LOUISE is really hitting the bottle now. ANNIE gets her things together in preparation for collecting her daughter.

LOU: The core of it is…they don't know who they are, so they project all their angst on us. They swagger like they are in a looped Tarantino and then we prop up their arrogance, we drop our knickers and we applaud their arrogance… because it's so…cock…and after numerous bottles of wine…so damn irresistible. But eh turn it around, when a woman behaves like that, it's laughingly ludicrous…it is my behaviour that really turns my stomach Annie…it

turns me…MY SELF-LOATHING CAN'T GET ANY
WORSE /

ANNIE: Come on…come on Louise…look don't…indulge
and /

LOU: Should be a deputy head by now, but not. However still
good for a girl from the grubby ghetto and getting out of
the ghetto is enough for one lifetime la la la. Still keeping
up. My undercover lover and I, I believe have finally
mutually parted for ever whatever…it's all cool…all good
man… And I am pregnant by /

ANNIE: Do we have to keep on using the word bastard?

LOU: IF I REALLY HATE MYSELF: IF I GO WITH THAT,
I'LL GET THROUGH, I WILL GET THROUGH.
DON'T YOU UNDERSTAND, DON'T YOU, DON'T
YOU?

ANNIE: …of course…I understand…I do know about being
a /

ANNIE exits.

LOU: I used to read this story in the *Second Sex* about this
woman who was forty-nearly like me, divorcee unlike me /

ANNIE: (*Offstage.*) …do you think I am in your sixth form? Do
you think I don't…

LOU: …who worked all day right to support her three kids
and her ageing parents. Still attractive, she had absolutely
bugger all time for playing the social game, the bullshit that
goes with making something…happen. However being a
woman with strong feelings, she believed in her given right
to satisfy those passions, to be a…woman. So kids in bed,
grandma and grandpa asleep, she would roam the Paris
streets and pick up men and be…passionate.

*ANNIE returns with her coat on, gets her bag, car keys in
hand.*

ANNIE: Silly cow /

LOU: One night after spending about an hour or two in a thicket in the Bois de Boulogne, her lover of the then moment, restrained and refused to let her leave. He wanted her name and address, he demanded to see her again, he wanted them to shack up, live together, babies and the works...or so he said... When she refused, he beat her and he beat her and left her fighting for her life.

ANNIE: What, do you think Jim?

LOU: Of course not...blood on his crisp clothing...now that doesn't look nice.

Beat.

ANNIE: So cutting to the chase /

LOU: Freedom and an attempt to combat loneliness on your birthday...always comes at a price...still /

ANNIE: Well thanks for that Germaine. (*Beat.*) I am going to meet my daughter. I'll call you later...we will talk more... later. (*She goes and kisses her.*) Love you darling...love you...love...it will be...it will be alright...mate!

Blends to a bar. LOUISE drinking as always alone. ANNIE should be seen in background, waiting for her daughter, at the school gates. JIM enters, taking off his earphones and putting away his iPod.

LOU: You are forty minutes late /

JIM: Security alert /

LOU: ...grateful for the crumbs of your time /

JIM: Yeah well you made yer point.

LOU: Do you want a drink...a coffee?

JIM: I haven't got long /

LOU: I don't want to suck you off /

JIM: You're very angry… it's only eleven o'clock /

LOU: It's half-term /

JIM: Do you always get angry in half-term?

LOU: I don't usually go into bars at eleven o'clock, but I bet /

JIM: What?

LOU: French fags though… Cliché…cliché…big /

JIM: Look if you called me here…just to ridicule me…I'll go now and /

LOU: How's your art…artist?

JIM: Stressful /

LOU: Did you finish your film…the one about Muslim boys on da estate?

JIM: …finances…people pulling out /

LOU: Shame you didn't…pull out /

JIM: What do you mean /

LOU: No worries.

Silence.

JIM: How's the?

LOU: It's shit at the moment…my work…teaching… everything's /

JIM: Sorry to hear that /

LOU: What?

JIM: Sorry to hear that /

LOU: I am going to get us a bottle of wine.

Blends to FREYA's school gates. FREYA enters.

ANNIE: Thought you would want a lift, came to meet you /

FREYA: Why do you want to keep on collecting me all of a sudden?

ANNIE: How was it?

FREYA: It was a resit, a resit…what else is there to say /

ANNIE: Well how do you think you did?

FREYA: I DID – END OF – I DID.

ANNIE: Fancy some retail therapy?

FREYA: What you offering this time /

ANNIE: Go into the West End?

FREYA:

ANNIE: We could drive out to grandma's and I could take you shopping at /

FREYA: Do I look like a chav?

ANNIE: What's wrong Freya…what's… I am only trying to /

FREYA: …this is my life and I have to sort out things /

ANNIE: What are these things?

FREYA: Things in my head, things that have started /

ANNIE: Things that Lucy's mother started /

FREYA: I don't want to talk about this alright, alright mum, alright?

ANNIE: 'Cause you can talk to Lucy's?

FREYA: Sometimes it helps to take it outside of the family /

Silence.

ANNIE: So no coffee even?

FREYA: Stop jacking my time…PLEASE MUM PLEASE.
Look why don't you call Louise or see one of your other

...friends? If it's okay, I need to be not with you. These thoughts are not for you, they are not for /

Blends to FREYA *walking off and* ANNIE *alone.* LOUISE *returns.*

JIM: I want to put you in the picture.

LOU: It's okay /

JIM: I can't get into...anything.

LOU:

JIM: This might sound er...I have to keep...let's say...vision, purity of vision...yeah? It's all I have as a...yeah...this two point four stuff man, well it...well it just...

LOU: I called you because /

JIM: There's no easy way to say it, there never is, but, but, but ...I don't want: I can't do anything...with anyone. I can't dilute myself any more man yeah? Not at the moment and I am sorry if this is a bit brutal and... My work is er...you think I'm a /

LOU: When you started crying about your ex in bed /

JIM: I'd rather it, if we avoided that messy...subject...look lots of women...

LOU: I saw your photo on *Guardian Soulmates*...your profile was ...interesting. (*Beat.*) London is just a series of moments innit?

JIM:

LOU: Don't want you either see...but don't get up...there is something else...something you must listen to...

Beat.

JIM: Have you got a light?

LOU:

He looks at his phone, sends a quick text, reluctantly faces LOUISE.

JIM: Where is this all going then?

LOU: I had an alright time with you...I fancied you /

JIM: Thanks /

LOU: I am responsible for my own behaviour...it was a laugh /

JIM: Just a laugh?

LOU: You are man...ly, although the lack of...

JIM: Yeah...well.

LOU: Not letting yourself go /

JIM: Now you're starting to /

LOU: Rock star, intellectual status, but age Jim...age?

He runs his fingers through his hair.

JIM: What?

LOU: ...good dress sense...I like yer style boy /

JIM: What do you really want?

LOU: ...attractive still...in a cool screw you up kind of way
...for a young girl in their desperate to get on, twenties
kind of way...an emotionally retarded kind of way...a
character that holds you in a novel /

JIM: AND?

LOU: ...yet can never in life. Sorry you may be thinking I am
veering to a bunny boiler...late eighties flavour (*Beat.*) I am
not...believe me I'm not...well I have due reason to be a
bit...I have /

JIM: Look I should be working...I've got loads... (*He looks
at her glass.*) Perhaps it would be good if you spoke to

someone, lots of people these days…addiction. I've had …have issues, but I /

LOUISE looks at her glass.

LOU: I know I shouldn't be boozing…women in the States in my condition could be locked up for that…but what the…it's all going down the toilet…today…it's really hitting me…really hitting me…more and /

JIM: What's hitting you?

LOU: It was generous of you to come…in all senses /

JIM: So?

LOU: I'm pregnant. It is yours…I know we had an accident. I took the morning after, however some divine intervention…means that this little bugger can't be stopped. So it's yours…it's yours…DADDY JIM!

JIM: Look /

LOU: I am not going to have it.

JIM: You're not?

LOU: How relieved is you? (*Beat.*) Well…I don't want a kid on my own…know the difficulties that Annie has been through…what sort of life would it really have and er it's too late in the game for me to start rethinking my life… It's not who I am Jim, it's not…was that explanation good enough for you?

JIM: Can I say anything?

LOU: Did you meet anyone special on-line?

Blends to ANNIE catching up with FREYA.

ANNIE: Talk to me darling…and don't run off when I am trying to have a conversation with /

FREYA: Why would I want to talk to you /

ANNIE: 'Cause I am your mother…I am /

FREYA: My mother and not my best friend /

ANNIE: Why are you being so nasty, it doesn't /

FREYA: Most people at school their parents are separated, they all have lots of step-mums, step-dads, it can be really confusing at times…but they know them, they know who they are…Lucy says it must have been something really bad between you, or he must have been a terrible terrible person. I told her I wrote to him once when I was eight and then thirteen but he never replied, and that you had suggested writing again… I don't know mum, I don't know… Even if he is and was a…arse, I think I want to start loving him…loving him mum, loving…being his …daughter?

FREYA sits with her mother. Blends to:

JIM: You are a very…

LOU: Fancy switching chairs then?

She laughs, he doesn't.

…look at the egg on my face now Jim. Your sense of humour was what drew me in.

JIM: Have you told anyone else?

LOU: Only…don't worry she's not in your business /

JIM: So your mind's made up?

LOU: I would like you to contribute.

JIM: I am going to go.

He attempts to exit.

LOU: It's all set up /

JIM: I…

LOU: ...thought I was some kind of feminist...for whatever that sells at now /

JIM stares.

I don't believe in orthodox religion...but I do keep thinking Jim...I do keep thinking...

JIM:

LOU: ...very primitive sense of fear and loathing at what I am doing...

JIM: I don't understand /

LOU: Will retribution surely follow? (*Beat.*) Roughly about four hundred quid. (*Big beat.*) Halves?

JIM: ...you want a cheque?

LOU: Is there hope in your film?

JIM: Have you got support?

LOU: Annie /

JIM: Have you told her?

LOU: Not in your business /

JIM: There's no one to tell /

LOU: ...if you would rather have a beer?

JIM: Have you told your mother?

LOU: What my real mum?

JIM: You're...the one that brought you up /

LOU: She's too old and I have never wanted to disappoint her. (*Beat.*) I'll just get on by and do it.

JIM: Did you ever want to be a...

LOU: Maybe if I am a romantic, it is a right man issue, but this, it just isn't right. IT SO AIN'T RIGHT IS IT?

She waits for an answer, he can't meet her eye, he shuffles in his chair, runs his fingers through his hair, gains some composure.

My mum gave me up, so I don't owe bog-standard motherhood one... Going part-time and spending all my wages on childcare... Maybe I could legendary do it all: have it all– maybe I am just a selfish bitch, who needs a good slap? This has to stop now Jim, please stop...

JIM: I used to quite like the idea of being a dad, y'know watching them play sport sort of stuff, taking them fishing, having a clever fucking kid, but it never happened man, never quite worked out like that and I suppose it never will now and er /

LOU: It's not the time for a debate here?

Silence. Big big silence. He coughs. She stares at him.

I am a survivor.

JIM: It was a good party.

LOU: A friend of a friend eh?

JIM: I wasn't going to, then I thought why not.

LOU: Got you off the computer...

JIM: Not really...I met this /

LOU: Did she taste sweet?

He moves his chair.

JIM: Her skin was clear, her flesh was firm and she had just finished her PhD at nineteen...is that what you want to hear Louise?

LOU:

JIM: Look I will send the money /

LOU: I mean you own your own flat, you can afford it. Thank you for not questioning me...thank you for believing me /

JIM: What?

LOU: I knew you wouldn't call me a liar…most…from before…would in this situation…wouldn't they?

JIM: So what do I end as?

Lost to herself, remembering.

LOU: …thanks for living up to my expectations…I appreciate that. (*Beat.*) You blink a lot don't you? Don't you eh?

He leaves. Blend to ANNIE's flat. LOUISE is staring into space. FREYA is getting dressed up to go out for the evening. FREYA is wearing a vulgar T-shirt, bought from Camden Market, and is playing very loud music and dancing as she gets ready.

FREYA: Mum can you come here please /

ANNIE: Okay what do you want?

FREYA: How do I look…these shoes or these boots /

ANNIE: You can't go out in that top /

FREYA: Boots or shoes?

ANNIE: Shoes and change.

FREYA: Why?

ANNIE: Because you are…portraying yourself as something… as something that you are not and /

FREYA: And what's that…mum?

ANNIE: CHANGE PLEASE NOW /

FREYA: Put some eyeliner on…for the girl!

ANNIE exits. FREYA sings along to the music, hoping LOUISE will applaud her show. LOUISE watches her, then just stares into space, playing with her hair.

Anything wrong Louise?

LOUISE doesn't respond. FREYA exits.

LOU: You look like you have seen a ghost /

ANNIE: I have. I have...I really /

LOU: What is it?

ANNIE: Wait till she leaves and I'll tell you /

FREYA: (*Offstage.*) What's this in the bathroom?

ANNIE: Just lie alright...agree to what I say...alright, alright? Am I loosing my mind...am I loosing my?

FREYA comes in with a pregnancy test.

ANNIE: It's Lou's...before you ask or go any further...it's Louise's.

LOU: Sorry...yeah can't really talk about it Freya...you don't mind do you...? Your top's er...a bit out there and /

FREYA: Er okay...sorry... Lou...sorry...yeah I'll think I might change /

She exits.

ANNIE: I am pregnant /

LOU: What are the odds for this...oh Mr God...what five hundred to one? What are you going to do then?

ANNIE: See my old priest, talk it over with someone who won't judge me, make my /

LOU: You can't have another child and /

ANNIE: ...seventeen... Seeing feet walk past the pavement above as I came round from it, in the basement and the light...I told myself then would never kill life again...never ever ever...

LOU: I can't believe I am /

ANNIE: Look you don't want children, never have and never will...

LOU:

ANNIE: I held Freya in my arms... A baby is a miracle /

LOU: It's not fair on you or Freya and I don't think it's fair on the child either...PROZAC P /

ANNIE: ...who has got back with his ex. Someone thinks he's alright... BUT I WILL DO IT ON MY OWN. (*Beat.*) I have been a good mother and I will continue to be a... good mother!

LOU: And continue to uphold the greatest cliché...it came in with vengeance after the Second World War /

ANNIE: I don't want a sociology lesson /

LOU:

ANNIE: It's nature, it's definite...

LOU: ...it is not nature that defines us women...duh!

ANNIE: And is that Simone again? Of course it must be, 'cause you've got all the time in the world to read. (*Beat.*) I respected your choice...now respect mine please?

LOU: (*Shouting.*) Idealistic /

ANNIE: ...no it's not and keep your voice down. Don't shout at me...like I'm one of your...fuck buddies... Your LOVER undercover or what or /

LOU: ...let's really divide ourselves up now...virgin and the whore big time...

ANNIE: I enjoyed every moment bringing up Freya: it was precious.

LOU: And the new contemporary reverence right for... motherhood...is all we have left of the family and look how well that worked...

ANNIE: ...you're not listening to me /

LOU: And you are not listening to me!

ANNIE: YOU NEVER BLOODY LISTEN TO ME, DO YOU LIKE IT WHEN SOMEONE ELSE SCREAMS AND SHOUTS...DO YOU...DO YOU?

FREYA enters, changed and moody.

FREYA: Lucy has just called, so I think I am going to meet her in the pub, is everything alright here, is everything okay?

ANNIE: Of course darling, of course /

LOU: Have a good time.

FREYA: Don't wait up for me...don't wait up alright!

ANNIE: Well how long are you going to be?

FREYA: Lucy and me might go off to a club. I'll probably text you, it's all not decided yet /

ANNIE: I could come and collect you...

FREYA: We will get a cab. I might stay at hers... I'm running late now /

LOU: Have fun /

ANNIE: ...love you...darling...love /

ANNIE waits for a kiss from her daughter. FREYA leaves. Huge silence. LOUISE sits next to ANNIE.

ANNIE: OH GOD, OH GOD, OH /

LOU: Some successful writer has adopted a child at sixty-seven. Despite being a multi-millionaire, success, fame it leaves you hollow...who loves you when the lights have gone down? Annie to me, in my head, it all seems such a spin. Never has having a baby been so...yummy. So yummy, mummy, yummy and such a...commodity /

ANNIE: I want you to be my friend, get under my skin Louise, BUT NO GO ON HAVE A DRINK, just have a drink mate and rant and rant and /

ANNIE places a bottle of wine in front of LOUISE, but LOUISE is lost in herself, working hard at her thoughts.

LOU: …all the disgusting things that are going on in this world /

ANNIE moves away.

ANNIE: You just don't care about me do you?

LOU: Ecological breakdown, over-populated and totally consumed earth…

ANNIE: …you sound like a mad woman, but eh…that's what /

LOU: So what did we all do? We went to fuck and make babies, those labours of our species' selfishness…those things that will get us an immediate return /

ANNIE: What page…what chapter is this from then?

LOU: An artist had a baby and just churned it out, NO PAIN, NO NOTHING. She went back to her sculpture two hours later. A picture in the evening paper.

ANNIE: Go home Louise /

LOU: It helped me as an actress, being a mother helped me as an actress…guess who said that one, guess who, come on …guess who…guess who?

ANNIE: I don't care /

LOU: IT'S EVERYWHERE AND I CAN'T BELIEVE IN IT. WE DON'T HAVE TO BE GOOD ANYMORE ANNIE, WE DON'T HAVE TO BE GOOD, THEY HAVE TO CATCH US WHILE THEY CAN, THEY HAVE TO /

Silence, then to herself.

The face of the bastard from before, MATT…all /

ANNIE: PERHAPS YOU DESERVE WHAT YOU GET, PERHAPS YOU DESERVE YOUR OWN LIFE LOUISE, YOU INVITE THESE MEN IN!

LOUISE finally stops and looks at her.

I gained some substance…I made sense yeah? My body made sense, my life made sense… Sometimes see I think you…hate…children. Babies who cry on trains, seen the way you look, mums who can't control their offspring… you just don't see it, you just don't get Lou /

LOU: Kids I taught five years ago still send me Christmas cards. Pupils need to talk to me…I want them: my students to be brilliant and strong. I want Freya to be brilliant and strong /

ANNIE: …maternal instinct though…you haven't got it /

LOU: …show me the science /

ANNIE: It's not in you…that primal, primal /

LOU: It's primal instinct to be violent…but we don't all act on it. And maternal / primal…

ANNIE: …no being…adopted…council estate… It's been so tragic hasn't it Lou?

LOU: I do know what it is to love, I DO KNOW WHAT IT IS /

ANNIE: Who do you love… COME ON TELL ME…WHO DOES LOUISE LOVE?

LOU: Do you just want to be even more immortal?

ANNIE: WHAT'S IN YOUR HEART? WHAT IS IN YOUR HEART LOUISE? WHEN DID YOU COME SO BLOODY RIDICULOUS? WE CAN'T CUT OUT OUR HEARTS, WE CAN'T, WE CAN'T. I DON'T BELIEVE IT'S A BASTARD WORLD FULL OF HORRIBLE PEOPLE…

LOUISE ignores her. Then blasts through:

LOU: Apply to be a mother to a special needs kid or an African child like /

ANNIE: Stupid /

LOU: Go and do some voluntary work with the youth…loads
of kids in the inner city gagging for someone to talk to.

ANNIE: The human race needs to go on.

LOU: The population is okay decreasing in the western
world… But in the developing world? Loads of kids need
homes…love…simple simple love.

Silence.

ANNIE: I see Freya desperate to get away from me, she has her
future /

LOU: Who's Lesbo Lucy?

ANNIE: When she leaves /

LOU: This is very earth mother /

ANNIE: OKAY, I AM LONELY LOU, I AM SO
OUTRAGEOUSLY LONELY, THIS LONELINESS
IS ME. THIS IS ME LOUISE, THIS IS ME. (*Beat.*) So
maybe I am like one of your girls, who have babies in year
eight, maybe I am no different, but this is me. I am going
to have this baby yeah and you have made me cry, happy
now, happy?

LOU: Oh get a fucking life.

ANNIE: …selfish bitch…not for being childless understand…
each to their own Lou…each to their own. You can't just
think what you want to think…YOU DON'T GET IT,
YOU DON'T BASTARD GET IT!

*Blends to: LOUISE visits MATHIEU. ANNIE alone. MATHIEU
enters.*

MATT: Look we will have to keep the noise down, I have just
got them off to sleep and Bessie's got a bit of a cold, so I
want her to have an unbroken night.

LOU: Sorry…I was a bit manic with the doorbell /

MATT: Now I got chicken curry, I'll have this. Some egg fried rice, chips. My girls love Chinese normally, but they would hardly touch any of it. (*He begins to eat and thus ignore her.*)

LOU: Do you always feed your children takeaways?

MATT:

LOU: Can we turn off the telly /

MATT:

LOU: I should not have called on you, but I needed a friend like, thanks for letting me in and /

MATT: What's wrong then …what is…what is it?

LOU:

MATT: Some wine or something for me /

He swigs back a glass.

LOU: I am going to go

MATT: But I thought you needed a friend…

LOU: I can't stay Matt, I just can't stay /

MATT: Relax yourself …come on…relax yourself Louise /

LOU:

MATT: Are you hot enough?

LOU: I didn't want to be on my own /

MATT:

LOU: Not tonight…I didn't want to be on my own tonight /

MATT: …a drink?

LOU: What?

MATT: …said have a drink…here /

LOU: That's your answer to everything /

MATT:

LOU: Did you like the present I bought for you…I know you have wanted that CD for ages, I hope you like it, I hope you do…I was so excited when I saw it in the shop, got to get that for Matt, Matt would love that /

MATT: I already have it…sorry.

LOU: Did you ever read the books I got for you…y'know the black history stuff off the internet and…

MATT: Always trying to educate me in your way…wanting to make me into somebody else and…nah…nah /

She gets up, proceeds to go to the door.

LOU: Please forgive me, for everything I've done to you, please, all I can say is…sorry, I am really very sorry and I miss you so much, I miss you so /

MATT:

LOU: However the hardest things you ever have to do, you have to do them on your own…yeah?

MATT: Has somebody hurt you, has somebody done something to you, come on tell us then?

LOU: I am one cunt, one lousy fucking cunt.

MATT: I don't like this, I don't like this one bit /

LOU: Sorry, sorry, I know your children…your /

MATT: WHAT OFF TO OZ?

She comes back from the door.

LOU: Talk to me about them, please talk to me /

She sits beside him.

MATT: Why do you want to know now all of sudden? Is it 'cause they are here, is that it…is that it Louise?

LOU:

MATT: So many times in the early days I asked you to meet them, but you never wanted to see them, you never wanted to meet my children.

LOU: You always said she would take them away from you /

MATT: Do you not really like kids then Louise and that's why you never wanted to meet them?

LOU:

MATT: Not good enough…not good enough at all.

Big silence.

LOU: So what are you going to do, when they have gone?

MATT: I'll see them what one time per year max…when I can fly out, they will forget me…call someone else daddy…

LOU: Course they won't.

MATT: It's blood and you don't understand that sort of stuff…

MATHIEU opens a can of beer, stares into space.

I was committed to her, I was man, I was. I was in love with her and I gave her babies: our babies, the things that women want /

LOU: Did you ever want to have a child with me?

MATT:

They look at each other, he swigs more beer.

See everyone who knew us said I was the decent guy: Mr Nice Guy and that's right isn't Louise and where does it get you…where does it get you eh?

LOU:

MATT: I smiled at her and then all of a sudden I am buying her a house. Never went out with the boys, then she found someone else, some Kiwi guy and she wanted me out of my own home. Now she is finally going, she has been planning it ever since the day, that spectacled…surfer walked into my family. I did nothing wrong man…I did nothing wrong… (*Big beat.*) And all I did was not make your party and here we are…HERE WE ARE…again!

Silence.

LOU: …you were a…saint…a ghetto…saint?

MATT: …don't think I am dumb.

LOU: I don't. I think I still love you.

MATT: No you don't…you don't love me, YOU DON'T LOVE ANYONE BUT YOURSELF!

LOU:

Big big silence.

MATT: I just feel like I've missed out on so many things in this…life…so many…everything's slipping away and trying to keep it all together but…it's all too late, too too late and…

She goes to him and attempts to hold him in her arms. He pulls well away from her.

LOU: It's alright babe…it's alright /

MATT: I just helped your image too, but never invited to meet the parents woman?

She breaks away, takes a fag and lights up, wipes her tears.

LOU: Maybe it's too late to try again…but I think we could Matt, I think we could.

MATT: Are you talking about yourself here…fuck…just wind her up and watch her /

LOU: It's always too late to get into something else…it's fear of…it was the logistics of having kids…but whatever it is…it is always absolute…fear…my fear…but maybe we could start again…

Silence. Suddenly children's voices are heard, and the sounds of 'daddy, daddy' comes flooding into the room.

LOU:

MATT: I've had a drink, I hate them smelling this on my breath, hang on a minute, hang on, don't go right, don't go… I HAVEN'T FINISHED WITH YOU LOUISE, I HAVEN'T /

MATHIEU exits. LOUISE picks up a child's toy and looks at it. She finds 'Alpha: Questions of Life' by Nicky Gumbel. She puts her head in her hands. MATHIEU stands in the door way, he has his sleeping daughter in his arms.

MATT: She's had a nightmare, she's back off again now.

He pulls his daughter close to him and kisses her forehead.

Come and look at her, come and see her, come and see my baby /

LOU:

MATHIEU can see she is visibly upset and he is staring at her.

We used to really need each other… What's all that about then? Who's God?

ANNIE's flat. FREYA enters, can't look at her mum.

FREYA: Are you…pregnant?

ANNIE: Yes /

FREYA: So what are you going to do mother?

ANNIE: I have to keep it /

FREYA: Because you kept me?

ANNIE: No /

FREYA: I don't want a baby in our flat /

ANNIE: You have to understand /

FREYA: …if you bring a baby into here… I shall go /

ANNIE: Why are you being so unfair?

FREYA: Because if I got pregnant now…which would be the last thing on earth… I know I would not keep it…so why should you?

ANNIE: I spoke to this priest I…

FREYA: Grow up mother /

ANNIE: He said it takes forty days for a soul to be complete… after forty days a soul is there and…

LOUISE leaves MATHIEU.

FREYA: Well I won't be living here much longer, I'll be at uni soon… I'LL BE AT UNI LIVING WITH MY GIRLFRIEND /

ANNIE: Can't I even discuss it with you?

FREYA: Not listening listening mummy!

ANNIE: Freya!

FREYA: Because it's always been me and you: us in it together and it means what we did: what we went through wasn't special. I missed out on a family: a proper family… Like Lucy has yeah? And what her dad has given her, made her, shaped her…his influences. Now you are going to do it all over again, because it's what you do mum. I thought I was special: a sacrifice: but no: it's just something you do: to fill… I do love you and do want to thank you for what you have…done…it's just I don't want to be in a family of freaks: a family of losers and you shouldn't be having this conversation with your daughter. YOU SHOULDN'T BE HAVING THIS CONVERSATION WITH YOUR DAUGHTER. If you have the child, you lose me…you lose me…decide mother (*She screams in ANNIE's face.*) Decide, decide MOTHER!!!

ANNIE slaps her daughter's face, they fight, ANNIE wins, FREYA storms out distraught.

ANNIE:

LOUISE walks onto the set of JIM's film.

JIM: I don't know what you want me to say /

He drags her to a corner out of view of his crew.

LOU: I did it /

JIM: I assume you did, and are you completely mad or, coming here and how did you know where I was and /

LOU: My life is going to be more anarchic and a hole and the devil will insert himself…

JIM: Come on /

LOU: One in three pregnancies end in an abortion in London and why do you think that is Jim? (*Beat.*) Do you want a receipt…James?

JIM: God Louise…you're /

LOU: I'd catch me whilst you can… I'd catch me whilst you can babe.

JEAN enters in a ray of light, almost mythical, the world stops.

JEAN: Now what's going on here, it's okay mummy's here, mum's here to listen…that's what mums do…that's what mum's were made for…I mean yer die for your kids… wouldn't you? It's alright, everything is going to be alright.

Blackout.

Act Two

JEAN and ANNIE alone in ANNIE's flat. JEAN is unpacking food.

ANNIE: Mum you don't have to do my shopping… I can /

JEAN: I bought some good stuff over at the market. Rice: six for a pound, tins of curry, sardines? Soup, biscuits, eggs, bread…some ham to take back for your dad. The fruit and veg is so cheap, lovely fish stall, man with the bad skin wasn't out with his flowers. I don't understand why you don't go down there more often?

ANNIE: I would do but, I just don't get round to it…mum /

JEAN: I mean the food is lovely in your supermarket, but you save at the market /

ANNIE: Mum is there something you are not telling me?

JEAN: So what do you want to do tonight girl?

ANNIE: Well Freya is going clubbing again and I thought we could get a takeaway and stay in and /

JEAN: I could put some of those pizzas I bought from home in the oven…just a bit of extra cheese. I've got that bottle of wine that dad sent up and /

ANNIE: Mum shouldn't have carried that on the tube /

JEAN: Well I didn't fall over did I?

ANNIE: Mum, you have got to stop doing so much, you really have… Mum why do you try and /

JEAN: Sitting about bores me /

ANNIE: You have to listen to the doctors… I want to know what they said.

JEAN: Should we invite Louise to come round tonight…should we eh?

ANNIE: I am not talking to her

JEAN: So what she done now?

ANNIE: Her mouth, I can't handle it mother…I just /

JEAN: You've been a good friend to her and she has been a very good friend to you too… She needs you darling…she needs you and /

ANNIE: Well people change…people do…they do /

JEAN: Life's too short lovely…life's too fucking /

ANNIE: She said I needed to get a fucking life /

JEAN: Well /

ANNIE: Don't say you agree with her mum /

JEAN: Well you do need to get a…job: something to do now Freya is older, you could retrain? I mean she shouldn't have said you needed to get a…fucking…life… I mean that is…harsh…but /

ANNIE: So you think she is right?

JEAN: What are you going to do darling…what are you going to be?

ANNIE: I have the aromatherapy and reiki…I mean it's a small business yeah…I am getting more clients /

JEAN: Hardly going to make you a millionaire and does it interest you really…does it…come on does it?

ANNIE: I like my clients and financially we are okay and yes it does…it /

JEAN: Daddy can't always give you money /

ANNIE: I don't sponge off him, he gave me the lump sum /

JEAN: Well better to have it while we are alive…than when we are six feet under. It's all a bit all over the place though isn't it babe eh? It's all a bit /

ANNIE: I don't think I will be able to get a full-time job /

JEAN: You live in London /

ANNIE: I know I live in London.

JEAN: If somebody can come over from…wherever…whatever and make something of themselves /

ANNIE: I'm having a baby mum /

JEAN: What?

ANNIE: It wasn't exactly…planned, it was an accident…but I have decided to have it and /

JEAN: …not all this /

ANNIE: Peter…but we are not even going there /

JEAN: Prozac /

ANNIE: My choice…me!

JEAN: How far gone are you?

ANNIE: Twelve weeks /

JEAN: Well then you can still…you don't have to have it…you don't have to /

ANNIE: I can't do that again /

JEAN: I think it's very…I think you shouldn't keep it…yeah I think you shouldn't /

ANNIE: How can you say that mum…how can you just say /

JEAN: I always wanted what was best for you…

ANNIE: Mum not now please.

JEAN: I said to myself when you were little…I thought…I don't want her to end up like me…not be able to do the things I couldn't do.

ANNIE: Mum: sentimental /

JEAN: All I wanted, was for you to be confident babe, have the stuff I didn't have and most importantly...have the education and the opportunities...that's all you want for your sons...your girl, your kids...opportunities for them to be /

ANNIE: And I thank you for that...but that's why at seventeen, you made me have an abortion and didn't allow me a /

JEAN: ...you were at college, going onto to university and it was wrong. The timing was very wrong, you were just a kid yourself.

ANNIE: You made the decision for me, I never got a single say.

JEAN shifts uncomfortably in her chair.

JEAN: I love Freya, I love all my grandchildren, people say you love your children, but you are in love with your grandchildren... And I think that's true...it is...it is. Now you are back in the game, women these days have so much don't they...you can see it, smell it, feel it...they have the...opportunities, the things we didn't have.

ANNIE: Mum, I know this, everyone knows this, why are you repeating all of this to me?

JEAN: I always wanted you to make something of yourself...I think you still can. I have always known you are... potentially brilliant and I want you to shine yet, shine as bright as /

ANNIE: So after all these years, being a mum hasn't been good enough, but it was good enough for your daughter-in-laws...mopping up the mess created by your sons...your darling boys. Really deep down all you wanted was for me to have a career...like Louise...eh mum...eh?

JEAN: You've done great with Freya, I am proud of you...but I want you to be proud of yourself /

ANNIE: ...why is my self-esteem such an issue for everyone?

JEAN: I remember sitting with my mum, the day before she died. It was a beautiful summer's day, the sun was pouring in and she had loads of flowers and cards by her bedside. Nanny was drifting in and out of consciousness, she didn't really know what was what, but I was sitting there holding her hand, and just looking at her face, my mum's face. I thought mum you have had twelve kids, twice as many grandchildren and then there's the great-grandchildren and it's just me and you sitting here mum. I kept on wiping her forehead, and looking at her. I watched her scrub everyone's floor well into her fifties, until she allowed her kids to support her at last. Nanny never had anything much, she never went abroad, first went into the West End when she was thirty. She was a beautiful, courageous woman, but she was made a martyr...she knew little else, now she didn't have a choice and she /

ANNIE: Sorry /

JEAN: I thought I would never get over losing my mum, I could never imagine the world without her, but I got on with things and I /

ANNIE: Mum, do you want a drink?

JEAN: Oh sod it, yeah.

ANNIE goes and gets her mum a drink.

When I passed my eleven-plus /

ANNIE pours her mum a drink.

ANNIE: You were two years ahead at school always /

JEAN: I was intelligent, the teachers said, you're intelligent Jean girl, you could have an academic future and I could sing, always sang, anywhere and everywhere. I had a lovely voice, sang in all the pubs, sang for /

ANNIE: Gangsters, with sequins in your hair...I know mum, I know.

JEAN: The night I met your dad, I had just done a few numbers and I was sitting at a table with all the faces, all the flashiness. I was just a bit of girl, too shy to say anything. Laughing at all their jokes, and I had this new dress that the woman next door had made for me. And there he was, hovering in the background, trying to catch my eye. Like your frock he goes. Not bold like the rest, or the bastard /

ANNIE: From before?

JEAN looks at her daughter.

JEAN: He could still hold his own mind, but I knew that man had an essence of quality. I just knew it. There have been times when I have hated him, but he still makes me laugh. Gets on me nerves, but makes me laugh and we have…it's what you choose to forget in a marriage that makes it work and /

ANNIE: Can you just tell me the truth please? YOU MUST TELL ME THE TRUTH MOTHER /

JEAN: I remember looking at you a day old and I thought she is going to have everything that a girl from hasn't…she is…she is…I always encouraged you. I said be aware…but I always encouraged you /

ANNIE: Dad made me fearless, physically fearless…well as much as he could but it was a man's world, full of boxing and football, full of geezers, lads, my brothers…your sons, even though I was at the better school…your sons…your darling boys…men, men, men.

JEAN: Annie /

ANNIE: My energy isn't that energy mum…I am different…I am…I am not that mum, and I am not…I don't want a plasma…I don't need a plasma television alright?

JEAN: (*Sighs and drinks.*)

ANNIE: Mum why were the boys always allowed to sit on the chairs, whilst I sat on the floor, when there wasn't enough chairs…you always said: boys you sit, you sit, boys, sit, sit. (*Beat.*) I wasn't strong enough mum to jump two generations… I am not my daughter mother. I am not Freya, and I don't know if I would really want to be. I had the education see but I wasn't strong enough to fight the…vile culture, couldn't be bothered enough to fight the culture…so I was, look, I am a mish-mash of many things, but I have made my choice mum and I will be a good mother again to my /

JEAN: Well Louise managed…to fight /

ANNIE: I am not Louise /

JEAN: No you had too much, too many many things, you haven't got her hunger /

ANNIE: I would hate to be Louise, I don't want her raw car-crash life…her life scares me…and you made me scared too…scared of men…situations /

JEAN: Well you got yourself pregnant at seventeen /

ANNIE: …eager to please…I watched you /

JEAN: I wanted you to be aware of the pitfalls in life and then give it your best shot /

ANNIE: I saw you…and don't try and reinvent things…

JEAN: IT'S JUST ALL BLOODY AND WHATEVER WAY YOU DO IT'S WRONG. YOU WERE IMMATURE DARLING, VERY IMMATURE AND NAIVE AND YOU STILL ARE, THAT'S YOU BABE, THAT'S JUST YOU. THERE'S JUST SOMETHING ABOUT YOU THAT IS SO UNWORDLY…SO /

JEAN starts coughing badly.

ANNIE: You alright mum, mum, let me get you a glass of water.

JEAN: Gone now. (*Takes a huge swig of whisky.*) How does Freya feel about all of this?

ANNIE: She's been a bit upset /

JEAN: Well who is going to tell dad... Me I suppose. I've done it twice before...should have written down the speech /

ANNIE: I can do this on my own...I can, I can!

JEAN: No you can't...you couldn't the first time /

ANNIE: ...so cruel /

JEAN: Well push me and I can be.

ANNIE:

JEAN: Is this why you have fallen out with Louise...what did she say about all of this?

ANNIE: She's just into herself mum...she's just /

JEAN: She's a good teacher and head of year and gets up in the morning, does a full week's work /

ANNIE: I GET UP IN THE MORNING, SHE HASN'T GOT CHILDREN.

JEAN is really hitting the bottle now, withdrawing.

JEAN: I just wish: that every time you get pregnant...I just wish...that the father was at least halfway decent, not a manic depressive, and not a violent...poet on a bike, who you have to run away from...when Freya is three months old and then he flees with another woman to the sea and she is in the family way too /

ANNIE: Well you really secured that Freya would never see her dad again, I mean how could he return after he'd been beaten senseless...left to die nearly...I knew the family got a contract out on him...the information filtered through to me, he got sent a wreath and then he was done over...

JEAN: You were being smacked about, you ended up in casualty, where's the poetry...where's the bastard art in that? You had no nose and four broken ribs, you had just had Freya, and he was using you as a football, even though he was this poet on a bike...that's what you called him... wasn't it darling?

ANNIE: Well that's what you do in the east of end RETALIATE and up the stakes and it all plays out like a trite film...but it doesn't make it right and that's why I am getting so much grief from my daughter now...for her being raised in a single parent family. Freya has missed out and I am choosing not to tell her all of this and how do you think that effects me eh... Eh? Covering up to my daughter and protecting my mother?

JEAN: You hurt my kids, I'll get someone to hurt you. Look, he wasn't somebody that was willing to stick around anyhow. He could have come back later, offered money, he didn't want to know...he was a C. And now Peter...the fathers have been hideous choices. You could have done better if you had picked them out of the hat.

JEAN starts coughing worse than before. ANNIE looks at her, goes and gets her a glass of water. ANNIE sits with her mum. A moment between them.

I am alright babe, I am alright.

Silence.

ANNIE: I saw my old priest.

JEAN: So what are you back on the old Catholicism now, not very Chi is it babe?

ANNIE: You used to believe...you brought me up to believe /

JEAN: Really think about this...don't get all organic and just say well I've made my decision...really really think...sod the priest...he's probably gay /

ANNIE: Mother /

JEAN: And what the hell do they know anyway...living a fantasy...indulging themselves. You outgrew Barbie... netball...you should of outgrown religion by now. His numbers are down, the church pounces when you are vulnerable...don't be thick Annie...don't be thick /

ANNIE: And what about the rights of the babe?

JEAN: It's a foetus, not a baby...twelve weeks is foetus /

ANNIE: And what about twenty-six weeks?

JEAN: They cry, they feel pain...they look like a baby.

ANNIE: Life mum life.

JEAN: I wish people really cared as much about what's happening to kids these days, as some care about embryos.

ANNIE: Sorry for being a huge disappointment.

JEAN: My little girl...my little girl...what am I gonna do with you, how will you /

ANNIE: I feel this urge to give birth to this baby...

JEAN:

ANNIE: I want it to see the world, London in the rain, to know you, to know dad and Freya and all the people I love... All the people in my...

JEAN: Come here.

JEAN holds her daughter, a tender loving moment.

ANNIE: Can you make me a cup of tea mum?

JEAN strokes her daughter's hair.

JEAN: I just haven't got the energy to look after another baby...I just haven't got the...women become invisible as they get older...they become...

ANNIE exits. JEAN sits alone in ANNIE's flat. JEAN remains visible for the rest of the play. Blends to somewhere green and open. JIM stares out.

JIM: This is still a fabulous city, no matter what anyone says, this is still the place to be and /

LOU: Yeah!

JIM: I spent a few years, sulking back home when my work wasn't getting made, but I had to come back, had to get over stuff. You can only do it here y'know, this is the place. Back home, everything's settled, here's where the vibe is and it's not a mono-culture like where I...I am a Londoner...I am a /

LOU: Y'know I am not after...

JIM: What are you after Louise?

LOU: My life.

JIM: Hope you catch it, hope you catch it hard.

More silence.

LOU: Have you not quite got an angle on me yet /

JIM: Something like that...something like that...well that was what you wanted me to say...yeah?

Silence.

Being adopted /

LOU: ...you remembered and let me see... You're making a film? (*Beat.*) And I could be one of the characters in it...yep? Prostitute one...tart with an enormous...heart?

JIM: ...cynical...how bloody cynical are you man...how can you think that of me... How can you... (*He shakes his head. Beat.*) Well I am actually...sorry...sorry...look sorry...it's not definite, not anything really...nothing, just... (*Beat.*) This guy I know, says it's an idea...something that the er…are looking for…look it's not anything yet…but… sorry…sorry Louise…yeah…I am a…

LOU: My mother was forced to give me up well… It was the World Cup or something and she said that they were going to put her in a mental institution, her words and that's why she had to let me go, and thank God she did. (*Beat.*) She was a bit of a nutter /

JIM: So it's in the genes?

LOU: I was twenty-nine when we first met, she had three other children that she'd given up for adoption too, I was in the middle… Her father never let her keep the children, she was always sent away and then returned without her child. (*Beat.*) She was living south of the river, it was filthy.

JIM: It was a different time /

LOU: My adopted mother said she didn't love me instantly but there was definitely a chemistry there. Lots of adopted people want to have kids, because they want to see their blood, whereas me…

JIM:

Silence. LOUISE gets a candle out of her bag and lights it.

LOU: …today I wanted us to remember the little life that we had between us…

JIM: I…

LOU: You drink far too much Jim!

He sits down away from her, studying her in detail as much as he can.

JIM: Do you fancy going away this weekend? I've got some friends, chilled people, they would enjoy you y'know, they have this crazy house in Oxford, just as friends like, me and you, I mean they would know we weren't a couple like and it could end in tears but eh if you promise not to kill a BAS- ...someone like me. Do you fancy it...do you Louise? How about it love ...babe?

Huge silence.

LOU: The war against terror!

JIM: What?

LOU: But our civilization won't end with some phenomenal terror attack y'know... It will end with the female population saying... What should I do with my eggs...I can't find a man...there's no spunk good enough...I can't ...nah leave it out!

He finishes off what she was going to say:

JIM: I can't really love...anyone. There's no love in me, I get you Louise, I get you.

LOU: I gave up trying to convince people to love me years ago, and therefore stopped really loving I think, so if I...

JIM: I understand you, believe me I do.

LOU: I got rid of my baby – LIFE OKAY? And I just wanted a /

JIM:

LOU: ...a man to listen to me /

JIM: And anyone to listen, anyone you can push your bristling honesty on, and hurt Louise, hurt. (*Beat.*) I think you underestimated me...I didn't give you much option /

LOU: Essentially you were cold in the morning and I like mine with a kiss, I like mine with a /

JIM:

LOU: You had swept me away the night before, asked me if my breasts were real and took me to look at the urban skyline...

JIM:

LOU: ...the dark endless sky and showed me the beauty you were educated enough to appreciate /

JIM: And then I kissed you /

LOU: ...and it was confident and hardcore and masculine and I sensed something...something possible...

JIM:

LOU: Was your ex really that horrible to you...did she used to hit you and draw blood?

JIM: ENOUGH, OKAY ENOUGH. THAT'S REALLY ENOUGH!

Silence. JIM looks up at the sun, feels its heat, then looks at the candle.

What a beautiful day, what a glorious, look at the light, just look at that the... I didn't just come here...because I wanted a story...it wasn't that exploitative or tiny...but it was about a need Louise...a fundamental...need...I am going to have to get this all out...have to get it all...out, out, fucking out man!

Silence.

LOU: I thought...I'd be behaving without even less self-control /

JIM: ...new bastards and all the bastards from before laughing...having a good old...ravaged by Satan...well you haven't been...have you?

LOU: No I'm just...

JIM: ...yeah...yeah...yeah.

Silence. He watches her. JEAN lights up.

LOU: A woman in the chemist had a bundle in her arms this morning, who couldn't have been more than three days old, I tell you I had to leave, I just darted out of there faster than…

JIM: You well and truly made your point!

LOU: (*Big beat.*) How's the current film?

JIM: Good, working well…I think it will pack an important punch…yeah 'cause it's nearly finished, well we are going into post-production…it's only a short…so /

LOU: Short /

JIM: Yeah…there is this kid, Hussain, he played the lead. Totally authentic, the real deal, the real real deal. He's really got something…special as a performer, his parents were violently against him doing my film, but I somehow persuaded them…somehow won them over…I am going to look after him you know, help him as much as I can, yeah…he's my boy, he's my /

LOU: Result. (*Beat.*) What do you want Jim…Jimmy…James?

JIM: I know what I don't want…I don't want this film to be a failure and it's a crucial piece of work, a kid died on the estate last week…he was a young black guy and only eighteen… He was attacked by a gang of young men of Asian or Arabic appearance…it's still out there man.

LOU: Tell me /

He struggles and we see his dilemma. He looks her in the eye.

JIM:

LOU: Well you are halfway there…do you feel free er /

JIM: To a degree…yes…look I had better get back to my work, back to /

LOU: Your life /

JIM: I deleted my profile y'know… I deleted… I deleted…

He kisses her on the cheek. A moment between the two of them and she gives him a half smile, he exits quickly. LOUISE blows out the candle. MATHIEU enters, another park, somewhere green. JEAN stands and faces out.

MATT: I can't stay long /

LOU: Hello!

He has a bottle of wine in a plastic bag and a football scarf.

MATT: I got it for you as a thank you /

LOU:

MATT: No you getting me that cheaper flight and being so helpful…here's the cheque and here's a…

LOUISE takes the football scarf and smiles.

Some geezer…some man…was knocking them out down the market, it's er…you don't have to wear it, it's alright you don't have to /

LOU: Did you speak to your children?

MATT: They are settling in alright, going out in a month, been buying them a few things /

LOU: It's a long flight…a long, long flight.

MATHIEU shuffles.

Is that a prospectus?

MATT: I might try and take a course in this er… fancy a change man, fancy a big big change. (*Beat.*) Do you know what I mean? Do you Louise do you…do you?

LOU: You have nothing to loose, nothing to loose at /

MATT: I'm not making excuses /

LOU: You are /

MATT: Here we go /

LOU: We are good mates and maybe that is all you can ask for in life. We have these things in our heads, what it's all going to turn out like and who we are and what we want… What we are going to /

MATT: So what are you saying to me?

Silence. LOUISE looks at JEAN.

LOU: Annie's pregnant.

MATT: Is she happy about that?

LOU: She wasn't speaking to me for a while, but now she wants to see me again, has even invited me over there for lunch.

MATT: Maybe she has got something up her sleeve, I mean haven't all women /

LOU: I will allow you that /

She looks at the scarf.

MATT: No you are a good friend…you never know what you've got until it's…

He wraps the scarf around her neck. She tightens it.

LOU: Are you seeing anyone Matt?

MATT: I have been going to a church and /

LOU: Why?

MATT: Children are gifts from above y'know.

LOU: (*Clutching the wine.*) Right /

MATT: We cannot expect them to always be there, they are not our sole property, they are on loan and that's all we can do, love them for as long as we can, as best we can. They are one of the ways that we really do get closer to /

LOU: Touching the face of God?

MATT: …in these…times…yeah…yeah /

LOU: Children help us remember what is important and er /

MATT: Yeah /

LOU: Don't loose your ability to reason /

MATT: What?

LOU: I think I've got to go.

MATT: Yeah me too…me…

LOU: …call you later…or you call me…CALL ME sometime yeah?

MATT: It's really good to see you, you don't know how good it is to see /

LOU: Whatever gets you through eh?

MATT: I didn't want to go via the courts, I mean it wipes you out doesn't it? I would have been financially finished. I didn't want to stop them from having a better life, growing up in the sun, all the nice stuff that goes with that, all the freedom, all the choices… She could give them more than me couldn't she? Couldn't she eh?

She touches the football scarf and laughs. She wraps her arms around him and envelopes him like a child. She strokes his head. He looks at her.

It will be alright, it will be…

She continues to stroke his head.

LOU: My baby, my baby, my baby Matt!

MATT: Look I got married okay.

LOU: What?

MATT: She's a Christian too, it happened quickly, over a couple of days…I had a baptism, it was a bit weird, kind of emotional, kind of… They do these meals at the church, and everyone is close and it's interesting, really interesting and…I have been reading about fragmentation of the… I feel closer to God alright? I feel closer to… It was a…epiphany of sorts…yeah a… Look, I want to be good, I want to do something decent and wholesome with my life…don't want to be Kwarme or Andy, chirpsing gals and shag and leave them…losing the plot every sordid weekend, NOTHING TO THEIR HOLLOW AND EMPTY EMPTY LIVES! I don't want to go out all the time anymore, I don't want to spray all my money in the clubs, I am not in my twenties, I am losing my hair for God's sake…I am losing my…hair! Want things to be just honest, I want things to be pure, I do want to have a family…I want a wife, kids and a family again, a home and a family…a family Louise a…a… She was willing to commit alright and she did, she did and although, I can't stop loving you and I can't stop thinking about you and you are so in my heart man and I know somewhere along the line, I am living in a nightmare…I am living in a /

LOU:

MATT: You never wanted me Louise, so you are not allowed to cry…you are not allowed to…

LOU: I want someone, I wanted a version of you Matt, you were in my dreams, I didn't imagine the future without you /

MATT: I wanted you, I wanted you, I wanted you alright and that's all I ever wanted! I was in love with you…I was in love with you…I was, I WAS UNDERCOVER, I WAS /

LOU: Bastard and you didn't even invite me /

MATT: Can I still text you baby?

LOU: No!

MATT: When I was inside you it felt like home.

ANNIE's flat. JEAN watches and sighs. LOUISE sits next to JEAN, who is again smoking.

JEAN: You should take better care of yourself…you really should.

LOU:

JEAN: I don't think she should have it…mum thinks she shouldn't have it…

LOU:

JEAN: How's you coping?

LOU: Jean have you got a fag please, have you got a…

JEAN gives her a fag.

JEAN: There you go girl. (*Beat.*) There you go and…

LOUISE lights up, shaking.

LOU: I'd love you to come and see one of my shows, I know I'm not a professional director, but they get great feedback at school and I have one on next week so if you /

JEAN: Annie is going to church regularly now. Getting back down on her knees and the church loves a woman begging on her knees /

LOU:

JEAN: Saw too much…seen too much me and sixty-five: not long now…not long /

LOU: Don't say that…don't say /

JEAN: I don't like the way the world is changing, too greedy: too fast and abnormal and greedy. Everyone keeps telling us it's evolution, but the Muslims don't seem to have to evolve…and I wouldn't bring kids into this…I wouldn't. I wouldn't! We were happy we had enough to eat. Freya, like two of my other grandchildren asked for an iPod or something ish for Christmas. I used to ask for a holy

statue…wonder what the new baby is gonna ask for…
IRELAND?

LOU: Why are so against this one Jean?

JEAN: …you will be there for her darling, she's going to need
you, don't say anything to her just yet, just be kind Lou, be
a good friend and be kind. You will do that for me…won't
yer?

Silence. ANNIE enters, followed by a petulant FREYA.

ANNIE: Now we are all having…

JEAN: Freya help your mum…

ANNIE: ONLY A BOWL OF SALAD /

FREYA: Okay, okay.

*ANNIE, LOUISE and FREYA all work together at preparing the
meal. JEAN goes to the stereo, puts on some music. The intro plays
and JEAN stares into space. A spotlight comes up and JEAN is our
only focus. The current world is fading. JEAN starts singing to
'Cry Me A River'. We are back in the '60s and she is performing
to the faces, the gangsters, with sequins in her lush hair. Towards
the very end of the song, as the music peters out, LOUISE's phone
rings. We see MATHIEU from a distance.*

LOU: I'll let it go onto voicemail.

ANNIE: Anyone important?

LOU: He…

JEAN is pouring a huge whisky.

JEAN: …will he do?

ANNIE: He is what they – we call a…undercover…a fuck-
buddy mother, or am I speaking out of turn Louise, am I
speaking out of…

JEAN: Where do I get one of them then…where do I get…

LOUISE is visibly hurt.

LOU: He found his Jesus alright, he found his…

JEAN raises her eyebrows and laughs.

JEAN: And God fucking help him…and God fucking…I…

MATHIEU stays in the distance. FREYA enters.

FREYA: What's going on?

ANNIE:

JEAN: Well if we didn't laugh we would cry /

ANNIE: And all other clichés mum and all other…

JEAN: Too right darling…too right…nothing like a bastard cliché /

FREYA: Okay? Everything okay…is everything…

Huge silence.

Lucy she wants to go to Reading, she wants to do Politics… she is trying to convince me…I still want to do Art…but… what do you think I should do /

JEAN: You have got to believe in yourself Freya, believe in yourself…that's all we /

FREYA: I could see Lucy being a politician…but me I don't know that I really could, her dad helps her with her stuff see grandma. Her dad he is nice enough, but sometimes he gets really grumpy and the last time I was around there he didn't speak to me at all. He was playing music in his room. Her mother, she's always talking about herself, bigging herself up, why does she need to big herself up when she is already big, Latvia the nanny, did tell me that Lucy's mum once went into hospital for depression or something, but she's okay now…she is…she is…she really is… I've got this friend Keresha, tall, slim…she's been ringing me a lot, her family are not like Lucy's, her mum is on her third husband, she stills sees her dad, he plays in a band and has locks to his toes. She's got a brother Kurtis and he is fit bwoi! Yeah fit…Lucy says Keresha is boring, I don't think so…Keresha isn't as exam driven as Lucy that's all…that's… Keresha wants me to go to the Canary Islands or Cyprus with her and Kurtis in the summer, Lucy says Tenerife is for football shirts…and I will probably get stabbed in Ayia Napa…I don't know. It's a long time to the summer…a long /

JEAN: …her painting is lovely isn't it Lou? My granddaughter's painting is /

LOU: Annie was top of our class at college and she was always the one I went to…brimming with compassion back then /

JEAN: We paid for her education, despite me favouring me sons…supposedly, we paid for her…education /

ANNIE: If Annie…who is quite not dead yet…could speak for herself /

FREYA: Mum?

ANNIE: Have felt rough all week, cramps and some bleeding, which I wanted…well you all didn't need to know about that. Even if you bleed a lot, that does not necessarily mean that you are going to have a miscarriage, pain is much more of a sign. I didn't want to ask anything of you all, so I kept it to myself…kept it to my… Yesterday I really didn't feel well all day. My body ached all over and I couldn't even lift a cup y'know…but I was like in tune with my heart. (*Beat.*) I looked out the window and thought…if ever there was a day to…end…this was it…this was going to be it. Yesterday I was aware I had a miscarriage…nature responded. A tad heartbreaking and rather ugly… As I stood up…held onto the sink, sorry that's how I broke your bubble bath Freya…well it then just trickled down my legs…wiped it and saw it on my hands…mixed IT with my tears…but I'm okay about it… I am… I am… I really am… Thought you all might be pleased. I know it's something you all wanted…something you all wished

85

for…me…thought was for the best, although I believe we have all /

LOU: Annie.

ANNIE: In some ancient African tribe…well there is this myth, that when the women of the tribe all wanted a particular woman to miscarry, they somehow all got together and conspired to make it happen…spiritually like… (*Beat.*) I can pour a bottle of wine down my throat now and as my body is already getting back to normal and I am sure you would all like to celebrate. My mother, my daughter, my best friend… Let's have a little toast…a toast…to my…freedom? MY FREEDOM. It's all just waiting for me now isn't…all just there and waiting…life? COME ON THEN…MY LIFE…LIFE…COME ON…COME ON. CATCH ME WHILST YOU CAN LIFE…CATCH ME WHILST YOU CAN. I didn't actually take the morning after, because I knew from the onset, that if it happened well it…and – (*Directly to LOUISE.*) – I am not you and I am not – (*To JEAN.*) – you /

LOU: We should…celebrate, what we all have…our lives as they are…as they stand and the mess and the…

ANNIE: Omelette for you Louise? Being you're a…veggie? I mean you wouldn't kill a chicken, but you would kill a… That's the way she really likes her eggs mum… (*To LOUISE.*) Isn't it love: nice and burnt and crispy, all sizzling in the pan /

Silence.

JEAN: Just feel like getting…stoned. Wasted. Out of me /

ANNIE: Somebody say something. I mean if I burst into tears, I'd only be propping up a…

ANNIE has got herself very upset.

JEAN: Yeah, you would, you cunting would. (*Beat.*) I want a traditional good old East End funeral see, all the trimmings…all the…I think I would like a horse and cart, you know like the gangsters had and I want flowers: lots of flowers. You must go over the top with the flowers, YOU MUST, YOU MUST… A huge MUM in white carnations, as high as me…now that would do, and I would want it to go into the fire with me… Not going to be buried, want a cremation and don't want anything green, want solid good wood, with a bit of brass…lots of Sinatra, maybe Tony Bennett, but the classics must be played and maybe you could write something Annie, maybe you could…but I want it sentimental, IT HAS TO BE SENTIMENTAL…I want people to cry…I want my kids to cry and I want your dad to wear his best suit and look totally handsome… people must have a good time at the do afterwards, and I want the booze to flow…she had a good life they will say…shame she went a bit early…but she had a good… Look, I just want to go out as I should… So we had better sit down and really talk darling…really /

ANNIE looks at them all. LOUISE's head is down. JEAN goes for more booze. FREYA goes to her mum: they are reconciled. MATHIEU is still there. LOUISE goes to MATHIEU. She stares at him and has to walk away.

Act Three

Time passes. JEAN and FREYA watch telly together. ANNIE and LOUISE in a chic restaurant in central London. They are both seated on stools at the bar.

LOU: Are you really not drinking, come on just a little one… just have a…

ANNIE: No thanks Louise, no thanks…

LOU: I thought we should just have a meal: the two of us.

ANNIE: Bit too cool for school /

LOU: So are we…

ANNIE: Don't know about that…

LOU: Nah…nah…nah /

ANNIE looks at the expensive menu, and sighs. Big silence.

How's Jean?

ANNIE: It's just a matter of time now /

LOU: I always wanted her to be my mum y'know…

ANNIE: She's still attempting to do everything for everyone, but obviously she can't /

LOU: …sorry /

ANNIE: Freya is going to delay going to Reading if she gets the grades. She wants to have as much time with her grandma as possible /

LOU: I do appreciate you coming out thanks, Annie, thanks. Can I come and see your mum? It's really important to me…I have missed her /

ANNIE: Yeah, of course you…can…of course you can Lou…

Silence.

I am really busy with work actually, it's kind of thriving… it's all sort of taken off, I don't know what has hit me…I don't know what has…

LOU: I put some leaflets up at school, in the staff room.

ANNIE: Some women came…thanks, thanks a lot Lou.

LOU: I saw Jim's film y'know, just by chance the other day, caught it at the London Film short whatever… It was a bit grim…but he's certainly got something…he's certainly got… He knows his Islam, he's about two years too late, but he knows his…he is a director…so it was /

Silence. LOUISE's phone rings – a ring tone of the moment. She switches it off.

ANNIE: What are you going to be when you grow up Louise?

LOU: Everything /

ANNIE:

LOU: And you?

ANNIE:

LOU: I am going around the world on my own.

ANNIE: What?

Beat.

LOU: I love travelling and Matt married someone else yeah and is about to have a child and although he still rings me in the middle of the night and…

ANNIE:

LOU: …and well I thought I'd see more South America, more of Asia and who knows… No going to do some voluntary work in Nepal…have a few things set up and /

ANNIE: Sunsets, rainforests and Havana?

LOU: No, when I come back, then maybe then I might think about adoption or fostering...I don't know...going to do something... Going to do something personally very good...will make my life...have a...some time in the future...perhaps /

ANNIE: Are you alright?

LOU: I'm fine mate, I'm fine...I am so fine /

ANNIE: I met someone /

LOU: Where?

ANNIE: He came for a treatment, very unprofessional, but very...nice...he's only twenty-five, Spanish and loads of...energy. He is proving to be a welcome respite from...

Silence.

I haven't been in touch because I did not think there was much common ground anymore but...

LOU:

ANNIE: I think I will always love you /

LOU: Because I had an abortion?

ANNIE: You really don't know me do you...about twenty years on and off...and you really don't know...

LOU: I did do recovery for a bit and I went to grief counselling y'know, wrote a letter to my baby, it's all part of the process...I think I have finally came to the conclusion...

ANNIE: What?

LOU:

ANNIE: Well we all have our...

LOU: You never returned my calls?

ANNIE: I just couldn't summon any enthusiasm to work at the friendship...

LOU:

ANNIE: Shall we go through to seating area…have you looked at the menu, what looks good do you think? (*Picking up a menu.*) How about the er…can't pronounce it – no…I don't want anything with er…

Silence.

I have taken your breath away…sorry…sorry Louise /

LOU:

ANNIE: Catch me whilst you can…catch me whilst you…

LOUISE picks up the menu.

LOU: I have started eating fish, I have a few more options, and if I am going to have…well… They have no option but to be with a kiss these days…

LOUISE laughs at her own joke.

ANNIE: Do you think people change?

LOU: …do you think you are earning your mortality Annie?

ANNIE: Do you think we ever know who we are?

LOU: …if the world doesn't know who it is…then how can we…how can possibly we…oh come on mate, have a drink with me…please! PLEASE HAVE A DRINK WITH ME, PLEASE ANNIE, PLEASE, I DON'T WANT TO LOSE YOU, I DON'T WANT TO LOSE YOU, YOU AND YOUR FAMILY MEAN THE WORLD TO ME! THEY MEAN THE /

Blends to:

JEAN: …your mum was such an ugly baby

FREYA: Ah!

JEAN: …grandad couldn't believe she was ours. She looked like she had already done ten rounds in a boxing ring.

He went out and bought her all these dresses as soon as, so she didn't look like a monster...so that the frilly pink frocks...somehow would make the bruises on her face: well not show so much. It was the birth y'see...the forceps that had made her look like that...and you can never tell with a baby, what they are eventually going to turn out like. I mean you can't tell either way, boy or girl, it makes no odds. After about a week all the bruising went down, and she was lovely, she was beautiful...our pride and joy...love of my...

Love of my...

Love.

FREYA cuddles her grandma. JEAN kisses her granddaughter. Blends to:

LOU: Let's get a bottle /

ANNIE: Life goes on?

LOU:

ANNIE: Sounding like my mum.

LOU: Yeah.

ANNIE: Sounding like my mother, am I sounding like my bloody mother?

Lights fade. The two women smile at each other. LOUISE takes ANNIE's hand. They attempt to blend.